THE SHOOTING SCRIPT®

THE CONSTANT GARDENER

SCREENPLAY BY
JEFFREY CAINE

BASED ON THE NOVEL BY
JOHN LE CARRÉ

FOREWORD BY JOHN LE CARRÉ

INTRODUCTION BY KENNETH TURAN

A Newmarket Shooting Script® Series Book
NEWMARKET PRESS • NEW YORK

FIRST EDITION

10 9 8 7 6 5 4 3 2 1

ISBN-13: 978-1-55704-712-0
ISBN-10: 1-55704-712-X

Library of Congress Catalog-in-Publication Data available upon request.

QUANTITY PURCHASES

Companies, professional groups, clubs, and other organizations may qualify for special terms when ordering quantities
of this title. For information, write to Special Sales, Newmarket Press, 18 East 48th Street, New York, NY 10017;
call (212) 832-3575 or 1-800-669-3903; FAX (212) 832-3629; or e-mail info@newmarketpress.com.

OTHER BOOKS IN THE NEWMARKET SHOOTING SCRIPT® SERIES INCLUDE:

About a Boy: The Shooting Script
Adaptation: The Shooting Script
The Age of Innocence: The Shooting Script
American Beauty: The Shooting Script
Ararat: The Shooting Script
A Beautiful Mind: The Shooting Script
Big Fish: The Shooting Script
The Birdcage: The Shooting Script
Blackhawk Down: The Shooting Script
Cast Away: The Shooting Script
Cinderella Man: The Shooting Script
Dead Man Walking: The Shooting Script
Eternal Sunshine of the Spotless Mind:
   The Shooting Script
Gods and Monsters: The Shooting Script
Gosford Park: The Shooting Script
Human Nature: The Shooting Script
I ♥ Huckabees: The Shooting Script

The Ice Storm: The Shooting Script
Igby Goes Down: The Shooting Script
In Good Company: The Shooting Script
Knight's Tale: The Shooting Script
Man on the Moon: The Shooting Script
The Matrix: The Shooting Script
The People vs. Larry Flynt: The Shooting Script
Pieces of April: The Shooting Script
Punch-Drunk Love: The Shooting Script
Red Dragon: The Shooting Script
The Shawshank Redemption: The Shooting Script
Sideways: The Shooting Script
Snow Falling on Cedars: The Shooting Script
The Squid and the Whale: The Shooting Script
State and Main: The Shooting Script
Traffic: The Shooting Script
The Truman Show: The Shooting Script
War of the Worlds: The Shooting Script

OTHER NEWMARKET PICTORIAL MOVIEBOOKS AND NEWMARKET INSIDER FILM BOOKS INCLUDE:

Amistad: A Celebration of the Film by Steven Spielberg
The Art of The Matrix*
The Art of X2*
Catch Me If You Can: The Illustrated Screenplay*
Chicago: The Movie and Lyrics*
Cold Mountain: The Journey from Book to Film
Dances with Wolves: The Illustrated Story of the Epic Film*
E.T. The Extra Terrestrial From Concept to Classic—The
   Illustrated Story of the Film and the Filmmakers*

Frida: Bringing Frida Kahlo's Life and Art to Film*
Gladiator: The Making of the Ridley Scott Epic Film
Hotel Rwanda: Bringing the True Story of an African Hero to Film*
The Jaws Log
Kinsey: Let's Talk About Sex*
Ray: A Tribute to the Movie, the Music, and the Man*
Saving Private Ryan: The Men, The Mission, The Movie
Schindler's List: Images of the Steven Spielberg Film

*Includes Screenplay

CONTENTS

FOREWORD

JOHN LE CARRÉ

Why was this one so good? Why do I keep watching it and feel none of the usual alienation?

It was never my film. It was always Fernando's. One of my greatest joys, still, is to watch him spread his filmmaker's wings: the rail journey to Berlin; the aerial transition from the golf course in Nairobi, over the rooftops of Kibera slum, to the glistening sterility of London's Gatwick Airport.

It was Ralph's film, too. His Justin Quayle is so beautifully paced and so carefully reasoned that his passion, when it finally displays itself, brings my tears racing.

And it was Rachel's film. The opinionated, wealthy young woman who is at first sight Justin's unruly child, then his irritatingly undiplomatic wife, becomes by stages his teacher, guide, and ur-woman. When Tessa pleads with Justin to take her with him to Africa, she tells him that, if he doesn't know her, he can learn her. And learn her he does, although not until she's dead.

Under Fernando's direction, the Tessa-Justin love story, Tessa's martyrdom, and Justin's journey of atonement are all to my eye beautifully drawn. The opportunities for kitsch were lurking at every corner, but Fernando missed them all.

It was also Jeffrey's film. Jeffrey Caine's script, like all scripts, was a moving target. The first time he wrote it, we had no director. The second time, we had a director and lost him. Then Fernando came aboard. Yet through numberless rewrites and fixes, Jeffrey never lost his determination, or his freshness. If it had been me, I would have thrown in the sponge. And the script would anyway have been no good.

And from Day One it was Simon's film. Simon Channing Williams, our unsung producer, had one objective only: to bring together all these *elements*, as we must call them, to make the best film they could, without compromise, without bending to commercial forces, which these days are anyway no longer commercial. For three years our backers came and went, but Simon's smile never faded; neither did his conviction that the man, the hour, and the money would finally come together. And magically they did.

Above all, it was Africa's film. From the moment Fernando came aboard, Africa was his leading character, his most affecting, most loveable, his saddest and most beautiful. Those who, like myself, had waited heart-in-mouth for echoes of the love and anger that drove *City of God* did not have to wait long. Fernando and his cinematographer, the rightly celebrated César Charlone, had worked in Africa before: in the violent barrios of Rio, where the despised descendants of Brazil's unnumbered African slaves lived out, and frequently ended, their brief lives. In the slums of Nairobi, Fernando found the same tragic juxtaposition of poverty and beauty, and the same unpardonable waste of young human life.

And if all these plaudits read too much like a jacket blurb, forgive me: I love this picture.

—January 2006

INTRODUCTION

KENNETH TURAN

John le Carré has been a writer of literate thrillers almost as long as Brazilian director Fernando Meirelles has been alive. He is a master novelist of the traditional school, while Meirelles, witness his Oscar-nominated *City of God*, has a jumpy, edgy, ultramodern filmmaking style. Their methods shouldn't mix, but in *The Constant Gardener*, assisted by superior acting by Ralph Fiennes and Rachel Weisz and an outstanding supporting cast, they've joined forces to create a film that grips us dramatically, intellectually, and emotionally.

As it turns out, the novelist (whose work was translated to film by screenwriter Jeffrey Caine) and the director have several things in common, including powerful storytelling gifts and the will to make a difference in the world. For if le Carré's concern with the unhealthy influence of multinational corporations makes *Gardener* an unusually meaty thriller, he is matched by Meirelles's passion for socially committed and intrinsically dramatic filmmaking. Their collaboration results in an intricate yet intimate piece of work that is disturbing for all the right reasons.

In addition to unfolding a mightily affecting love story wrapped in a complex whodunit plot, *The Constant Gardener* poses some stimulating questions. In a world where complicity in chicanery is the rule, what does it take to make a difference? What is the price individuals must pay for their idealism? And where market forces rule with an iron hand, what is the cost to society for being in thrall to unbridled corporate lust for profit?

Like the novel, Meirelles's film (smartly edited by Claire Simpson, an Oscar winner for *Platoon*) goes back and forth between the present and the past, as Fiennes's midlevel British diplomat Justin Quayle, characterized by le Carré

KENNETH TURAN is a *Los Angeles Times* staff writer.

as "a Foreign Office plodder," investigates the suspicious death of his impulsive and unstoppable wife, Tessa (Weisz), an activist firebrand who was everything he is not.

Le Carré, no one needs to be told, is completely at home in the world of duplicity, betrayal, and behind-the-scenes intrigue, and the film continually benefits from having his densely plotted novel and its textured adult characters as source material.

And because Justin, by virtue of his personality and the complexity of his quest, is initially well over his head in his investigations, his mental state is a good match for the disorienting visual style Meirelles and cinematographer César Charlone create. Using hand-held camerawork to create intimacy, Charlone enables us to connect on a visceral level with Justin's confusion, his sense that what he needs to know is just out of reach.

The cinematographer, Oscar-nominated for *City of God*, also does a remarkable job capturing the vivid, overcrowded crush of chaotic Africa. *The Constant Gardener* was photographed with some difficulty in Kenya, where it takes place, and scenes caught on the fly in Nairobi's Kibera, a staggering shantytown of 800,000 to 1 million souls, connect us indelibly to this unnerving, unforgettable side of the country.

Though the film starts with his wife's savage murder, Justin and Tessa's story begins not in Kenya but in England. They meet cute at his boring London lecture about foreign policy, where she, in an adroit bit of updating, lashes out at him as the representative of a British government that has sent troops to Iraq. She apologizes afterward for being rude, he calls her impassioned, and they fall into bed almost at once.

Justin and Tessa are not the easiest characters to convincingly animate, but the passion and skill Fiennes and Weisz bring to the roles make it happen. Because these two are so finely drawn and so splendidly acted, we never doubt their reality, never doubt the strength of their polar attraction. She feels safe with him, he enjoys being flummoxed by her, and when he tells her he is being posted to the British High Commission in Kenya and she is wild to go along, it feels inevitable that he will agree.

It's hard to think of an actor other than Ralph Fiennes who could bring Justin's mixture of timidity and attractiveness so convincingly to life. A career diplomat who goes where he's told—"like a Labrador," someone witheringly says—Fiennes's Justin not only radiates decency, consideration, and unfailing politeness, he makes those qualities sexy. Until he meets Tessa, the only outlet for his considerable energy and passion is meticulous gardening.

Completely inhabited by Weisz, Tessa has the kind of personality that could make even Gregor Mendel forget about his plants. It is perhaps the most fully realized performance of her career. Tessa—a woman who burns about injustice and believes that the world could be changed if people cared enough—has no difficulty speaking truth to power and sticking her nose in places, in this case the shenanigans of certain international companies, the establishment wishes she wouldn't.

(Part of Tessa's vividness stems from her basis in a real person, Yvette Pierpaoli, a friend of le Carré's and an advocate for Refugees International who died in a car accident while doing work in Kosovo. Both the novel and the film are dedicated to her as someone "who lived and died giving a damn," and le Carré has written with great feeling that "Tessa's commitment to the poor of Africa, particularly its women, her contempt for protocol, and her unswerving, often maddening determination to have her way stemmed quite consciously, as far as I was concerned, from Yvette's example.")

Justin is understandably shattered by Tessa's death. More surprisingly, he is radicalized by it. He ignores rumors of infidelity and remains determined, despite pointed warnings that "there are some very nasty things under rocks, especially in foreign gardens," to find out what she was investigating and why she died.

The Constant Gardener concerns itself, more than anything else, with Justin's finding out, his getting of wisdom. Fiennes has described the film as "a retrospective love affair," and there is a lot of truth in that. The more Justin learns, the more his sense of loss deepens, and the more terribly moving his search becomes.

Though Fiennes and Weisz carry the lion's share of the film's emotional burden, *The Constant Gardener* wouldn't be a fraction of the film it is without expert supporting work across the board. Especially noteworthy are Bill Nighy as an impeccably bloodless pillar of the establishment, Danny Huston as Justin's oleaginous boss, Gerard McSorley as a bluff business tycoon, and Pete Postlethwaite as the mysterious Lorbeer.

The Constant Gardener keeps the book's somber tone, though it does add on a bit more of an upbeat ending. But let no one doubt the extent of le Carré's and Meirelles's social concern. Practically the last thing viewers see is the novelist's on-screen fusillade: "Nobody in this story, and no outfit or corporation, thank God, is based upon an actual person or outfit in the real world. But I can tell you this; as my journey…progressed, I came to realize that, by comparison with reality, my story was as tame as a holiday post-card."

You have been warned.

—August 31, 2005

THE CONSTANT GARDENER

screenplay by

Jeffrey Caine

Based on the novel by John le Carré

March 8, 2004

Revised Pink Pages 17.03.04
Revised Blue Pages 22.04.04
Revised Green Pages 30.04.04
Revised Yellow Pages 77.05.04
Revised Lilac Pages 14.05.04

FADE IN ON:

1   ***EXT. RAILWAY LINE. DAY***   1

To the accompaniment of musicians a community theatre group is parading along a railway line: a human train...

WIDEN TO:

2   ***EXT. KIBERA SHANTY TOWN, NAIROBI. DAY***   2

The railway runs past a tangle of one-roomed shanties, part of a mile-wide sprawl of temporary tin-roofed huts that are the permanent homes of nearly a million souls. This is an unofficial city-within-a-city with a population and growth rate possibly equal to Dallas, Texas. The procession, as it's designed to do, is attracting followers. They join the human train as it snakes through Kibera, like party guests joining a conga.

One of those joining, the only white face among the hundreds of Africans, is TESSA QUAYLE. Tessa is in her mid-twenties, a dark-haired Anglo-Italian beauty in an advanced stage of pregnancy. Though she is physically attractive, the truly striking thing about her is an inner energy which hints at a range of passions, a capacity for commitment fierce enough to govern a life.

CUT TO:

3   ***EXT. KIBERA. AN HOUR LATER***   3

FAVOURING TESSA now among the audience as the theatre group performs its didactic play.

The most important message in Africa, and the least welcome, is being put across as entertainment to the residents of Africa's largest slum. AIDS: how to avoid it, how to check if you're HIV-positive, what to do if you are.

A group of KENYAN CHILDREN runs up to Tessa. One of them presents her with a gift they've made for the baby she's expecting: a mobile. African animals fashioned from the slats of a packing crate, strung together with twine.

Tessa accepts it, clearly touched by the love and care that has gone into its making.

4   ***EXT. HUT. AFTERNOON***   4

ARNOLD BLUHM - a strikingly handsome black Belgian doctor in his early thirties - pops a pill into the mouth of a young AFRICAN MOTHER, who is bottle-feeding a NEW-BORN.

(CONTINUED)

4   CONTINUED:

REVEAL TESSA alongside him, cradling A NAKED ONE YEAR-OLD
BABY in the crook of her left arm, her right hand holding the
hand of a TODDLER. He has been given the mobile to play with
while his family's medical needs are seen to.

                    TESSA
          What are you giving her?

                    BLUHM
          The usual cocktail. The government
          clinic didn't have any Nevirapine -
          again.
               (to mother)
          Your baby has gastro-enteritis,
          Mara. I want you to breast-feed.

The mother calls something into the hut. A young African man
comes out in response. This is JOMO.

                    TESSA
          Hello, Jomo.

                    JOMO
          Hello, Mama Tessa.
               (to Bluhm)
          Doctor Bluhm. What is the problem,
          please?

                    TESSA
          You are sterilizing the baby's
          bottles, aren't you, Jomo?

Jomo frowns. Not his business. Woman's business.

                    JOMO
          My wife does this.

                    BLUHM
               (to Tessa)
          The problem isn't the bottles. It's
          the milk.

                    JOMO
               (proudly defensive)
          I bring milk home - every day.

                    BLUHM
          And Mara makes it go further by
          diluting it.

He gestures at a plastic water jerrycan standing in the hut
entrance. The water inside it, drawn from a standpipe, is
yellowish and opaque.

                                        (CONTINUED)

                         BLUHM (CONT'D)
              With that.

Tessa pulls a face.

                         BLUHM (CONT'D)
              If she's HIV-positive, chances are
              you are too, Jomo.

                         TESSA
              Have you had an HIV test, Jomo?

                         JOMO
              I must go to work now. I am helping
              to serve at the party tonight.

                         TESSA
              You need to be tested.

                         JOMO
              I must go. I will be late.

He runs off. Tessa and Bluhm move on, wilting in the
oppressive heat.

4A   *EXT. KIBERA - BRIDGE. DAY*   4A

Tessa and Bluhm are crossing a little bridge.

                         BLUHM
              You shouldn't be wandering around
              in this heat.

                         TESSA
              Stop fussing, Arnold. You're as bad
              as Justin.

                         BLUHM
              If you were my wife I'd tie you to
              the bed.

                         TESSA
                   (smiles provocatively)
              And then what would you do?

5   *EXT. KIBERA/NAIROBI STREETS. DAY*   5

Following JOMO cycling to work. We see him:

CARRYING THE BIKE UP A HILL, Kibera b.g. behind him-

RIDING ALONGSIDE RAILWAY TRACKS (CRANE SHOT)-

5   CONTINUED: 5

PASSING THROUGH A SMALL COMMERCIAL NEIGHBOURHOOD near Kibera:
little shops etc.-

ENTERING A BUSY URBAN THOROUGHFARE-

TURNING IN FRONT OF SANDY WOODROW'S HOUSE-

5A   **EXT. HIGH COMMISSION. DAY**   5A

-and entering the High Commission car park.

6   **EXT./INT. HIGH COMMISSION. DAY**   6

We see him showering, changing into a white waiter's jacket,
and so into the kitchen.

Sweating black faces here, preparing food and drink for a
party under conditions that would wilt orchids.

7   **EXT. HIGH COMMISSION. NIGHT**   7

Beneath British and Kenyan flags flying side by side-

A LINE OF 10 GLEAMING LIMOS disgorges its DIGNITARIES to a
British-hosted party.

Armed uniformed Kenyans stand guarding the building's
entrance.

VARIOUS STAFF POV ANGLES: shoulders, legs, hands as the
guests climb out of their cars and enter the building.

8   **INT. HIGH COMMISSION - KITCHEN. EVENING**   8

JOMO, now wearing white gloves and carrying a silver tray of
champagne flutes, pushes open the swing doors to enter a
cooler, higher realm where SOFT MUSIC is playing...

9   **INT./EXT. HIGH COMMISSION FUNCTION ROOM/GARDEN. EVENING** 9

VIA A SERIES OF TRAVELLING SHOTS

we move among the party guests with JOMO and his tray.

First he serves the ranking group. DR NGABA is being
introduced by the High Commissioner, PORTER COLERIDGE (56),
to SIR BERNARD PELLEGRIN.

Pellegrin is a senior civil servant in his late forties,
patrician in manner and background. Coleridge is a man of
hollowed, scholarly appearance.

(CONTINUED)

>   COLERIDGE
>   Dr Joshua Ngaba of the Kenyan
>   Health Ministry...Sir Bernard
>   Pellegrin, head of FCO Africa Desk.

Pellegrin shakes Ngaba's hand.

>   PELLEGRIN
>   May I convey Her Majesty's warmest
>   greetings.

>   NGABA
>   Please thank Her Majesty, Sir
>   Bernard. I trust she is well.

>   PELLEGRIN
>   In the pink last time I saw her.

Having served his drinks, Jomo moves on, and we with him, to

SIR KENNETH CURTISS and CRICK, who are with silver-haired
PHIL McKENZIE (57). Kenny Curtiss is a coarse, bearish man of
about fifty, a lifelong user and abuser of power, entirely
self-made. His man Crick is younger and of a more athletic
stamp. As Jomo serves:

>   MCKENZIE
>   (Canadian accent)
>   How many are we talking about?

>   CURTISS
>   Couple of dozen. I wouldn't worry
>   about it, Phil.

>   MCKENZIE
>   I am worried about it, Kenny. I
>   didn't fly all the way from Canada
>   for the sunshine. I could've gotten
>   that in Bermuda.

>   CRICK
>   We're dealing with it, Mr McKenzie.

>   MCKENZIE
>   You damn well better be.

>   CURTISS
>   Markus reckons it'll bottom out in
>   a couple of weeks. If it goes over
>   thirty I'll let you know.

>   MCKENZIE
>   No, Kenny. If it goes over thirty I
>   don't want to know.

...then away with Jomo, moving down by rank to SANDY WOODROW,
41 year-old Head of Chancery and second-in-command in Nairobi
- a soldier's son, not public-school-educated but affecting
the manner. Sandy is with TESSA, who tonight wears a
voluminous, vividly coloured African-style maternity dress,
set off by an antique gold necklace.

>   SANDY
>   You're driving me mad, you do know
>   that?

>   TESSA
>   Don't be tiresome, Sandy. I'm fat
>   as a sow.
>   (taking drink)
>   Thank you, Jomo.
>   (to Sandy)
>   This time next week I'll be nursing
>   a litter.

>   SANDY
>   Can I come and see you?

>   TESSA
>   (a laugh)
>   In Uhuru?

>   SANDY
>   (shocked, taking drink)
>   God, Tessa, you're not having it
>   there!

...but Tessa's response is lost to us as we move on with Jomo
to

A HUDDLE OF JUNIORS: MIKE MILDREN (25), MIRIAM (Sandy's
secretary) AND CURRY, a junior Australian diplomat.

TESSA AND SANDY - MILDREN'S POV

>   MILDREN
>   Gin in one end, the other end into
>   someone's wife. *Homo diplomaticus.*

>   CURRY
>   Quaff 'n' boff.

Jomo can be seen serving a group comprising GHITA PEARSON
(23, Anglo-Indian, in a gold sari), ARNOLD BLUHM and TIM
DONOHUE (59), S.I.S. Head of Station Nairobi: a tall,
cadaverous-looking man with sunken cheeks and a straggling
moustache; terminally ill and looks it.

                                                        (CONTINUED)

                    MIRIAM
          Servicing needy wives counts as
          hazardous duty, doesn't it, Mike?

                    MILDREN
          No pay allowance.

But Curry's focus isn't on Tessa; it's on Pellegrin.

                    CURRY
          Who's the oily bugger with your
          boss, Mike?

                    MILDREN
          Sir Bernard Pellegrin. Annual
          descent from Mount Olympus.

                    CURRY
          Wouldn't mind being a fly on one of
          those noses. That's how the real
          stuff's done, mate. Headline
          summits, top-brass drop-ins.
          Embassies are just pubs with
          flagpoles.
               (toasting)
          God save the Crown and Anchor.

Jomo arrives with his tray and everyone here takes refills.

POV SHOT as the CURTISS-CRICK-McKENZIE group crosses to
PELLEGRIN, COLERIDGE and NGABA.

REVEAL POV AS TESSA's. She's still with Sandy, but her
attention is divided. Sandy's is exclusively on her.

                    TESSA
          For God's sake, Sandy. The Kibera
          women drop their babies in Uhuru
          every day.

                    SANDY
          They're not the wives of British
          diplomats.
               (a beat)
          Does Justin know?

                    GLORIA (V.O.)
          Do you know, Justin?

REVEAL GLORIA WOODROW (37) AND JUSTIN, behind them.

JUSTIN QUAYLE - an elegant man in his mid forties - is an
anachronism: an Old-Etonian English gentleman surviving in an
increasingly democratized Diplomatic Corps.

                                                        (CONTINUED)

His voice is ever soft, his bearing elegant, his manner
courteous. Yet there is nothing affected about him, his
refinement being as natural as breathing.

                    JUSTIN
          Yes, I do know, and I support my
          wife's decision.

                    GLORIA
          Well, she's certainly dressed to go
          native. Tessa, we're all dying to
          know where you got that amazing
          garment. Not Kibera, one assumes.

                    TESSA
          No, Gloria, not Kibera.

                    GLORIA
          So colourful. One feels quite the
          drab by comparison. Sandy, dear,
          you've monopolized Tessa long
          enough. Give her back to Justin.

                    JUSTIN
          I was taught to share, Gloria.

                    GLORIA
          Toys, dear, not wives.
               (hand on his arm)
          Your Dr Bluhm's looking very
          handsome tonight, Tessa.

With this Parthian shot she leads Sandy away.

                    JUSTIN
          Thought Arnold was going up-
          country.

                    TESSA
          He is. Don't worry, he won't take
          me. I asked.

                    JUSTIN
          Good. And I'd be happier still if
          you stayed out of Kibera. Until the
          baby's born, anyway.

                    TESSA
               (patting her bump)
          Wait till I'm single again.

She squeezes his hand, then moves off to join GHITA, BLUHM
and DONOHUE.

                                              (CONTINUED)

                              TESSA (CONT'D)
                    Hello, Tim. Struggling through
                    without Maud tonight?

                              DONOHUE
                    One of her party headaches. I take
                    mine standing up.

                              TESSA
                    How manly of you.
                         (to Ghita, mock-Gloria)
                    Love your sari, Ghita dahling. One
                    supposes some dark-skinned cousin
                    must have sent it from Madras.

                              GHITA
                         (echoing the accent)
                    Ectually Jodhpur, dahling, where
                    one's riding clothes come from.

Tessa nudges Bluhm, drawing his attention to the A-group.

Bluhm nods. Seen them.

Donohue turns his head to see who has caught their eye.

                              BLUHM
                    Interesting guests, Mr Donohue.

                              DONOHUE
                    We usually manage to rope in a
                    Kenyan big-wig or two to our
                    bashes.

ANGLE - PHIL McKENZIE AND DR NGABA deep in conversation.

                              BLUHM
                    Health Minister's turn was it?
                    Who's that he's talking to ?

Donohue looks, shrugs.

                              TESSA
                    Thought you spies knew everything,
                    Tim.

                              DONOHUE
                    Only God knows everything. He works
                    for Mossad.
                         (to Bluhm)
                    Met Dr Ngaba, have you?

CONTINUED: (6)

> BLUHM
> Yes, at the opening of a new state
> of the art clinic. Without
> autoclaves for sterilizing.

Donohue laughs.

> DONOHUE
> Probably converted them into a
> Mercedes.

> TESSA
> I've never met an alchemist before.

> DONOHUE
> I'd forgo that pleasure, Tessa.

But, taking Bluhm's arm, she steers him towards the A-group.

Ngaba frowns at Bluhm's approach, sensing trouble.

> COLERIDGE
> Ah, Tessa.
>   (to Dr Ngaba)
> May I introduce you to Tessa
> Quayle, Dr Ngaba - the wife of our
> er, representative for aid
> effectiveness. And this is Dr Bluhm
> of *Médecins sans Frontieres*.

> NGABA
> Dr Bluhm and I have met.

> TESSA
> At the clinic without autoclaves.
> We haven't met, Dr Ngaba, but as
> you see, I know your work.

Ngaba looks to Pellegrin in mute appeal.

> PELLEGRIN
> Do you know Sir Kenneth Curtiss?
> Chief Executive of ThreeBees?
>   (smarmy smile at Curtiss)
> He runs Britain's most successful
> business here in Kenya. We're very
> proud of him.

> TESSA
>   (sweetly, to Curtiss)
> Which of the B's are you?

Curtiss looks darkly at her. Nobody introduces McKenzie.

(CONTINUED)

                         PELLEGRIN
              You were going to show us the
              garden room, I think, Porter.

                         TESSA
              There is one thing I'd like to
              thank Dr Ngaba for....

Pellegrin shifts uneasily. Senses what's coming.

                         TESSA (CONT'D)
              The free Nevirapine.
                   (to Coleridge)
              The manufacturers are donating it
              for HIV-positive mothers.

                         COLERIDGE
              That's good to know.
                   (to the group)
              Shall we, er...

                         TESSA
              Problem is it isn't reaching them.

                         BLUHM
              Some, but not all.

                         TESSA
              So we've been wondering: is that a
              standard cock-up, Dr Ngaba, or were
              the pills converted into that limo
              you arrived in?

JOMO returns with his drinks tray at this point - receives a
headshake from Coleridge - moves on.

TRACKING WITH JOMO INTO THE GARDEN...where JUSTIN is now
chatting to some JUNIOR DIPLOMATS' WIVES.

As Jomo arrives so does SANDY. Butting in front of Jomo and
with an excusing gesture to the wives, Sandy pulls Justin
aside.

                         SANDY
              For Christ's sake, Justin, you've
              got to do something about Tessa.

                         JUSTIN
              What would you like me to do?

                         SANDY
              She's embarrassing our guests. Her
              and that bloody Bluhm. There'll be
              hell to pay, I can tell you.

He indicates. But we see that the A-list group has at last succeeded in freeing itself of Tessa and Bluhm and is heading *en masse* through French doors to the garden room.

> JUSTIN
> The squall seems to have passed.

> SANDY
> If you can't control her you should
> keep her locked up.

He swivels, touched suddenly on the shoulder from behind.

REVEAL CRICK

> CRICK
> They want you in the garden room,
> Mr Woodrow.

ANGLE ON GARDEN ROOM, where PELLEGRIN, COLERIDGE, McKENZIE, CURTISS AND NGABA - an exclusive caucus of five - are drinking champagne, smoking cigars and talking business.

Justin watches as Sandy is taken through the French doors by Crick to join them.

JUSTIN'S POV - TESSA AND BLUHM talking earnestly.

ON JUSTIN - excluded from both worlds. He looks into the garden. His gaze finds a Yellow Fever tree.

9A   **EXT. PLANT NURSERY. DAY**   9A

Justin and Gloria Woodrow, Sandy's wife, are examining a flowering shrub.

> JUSTIN
> No, I don't think so, Gloria. That
> hibiscus is going to get too big
> for the front of your border. In
> any case, I think you've probably
> bought enough.

She glances back at a trolley loaded with the plants she has bought and that Justin has helped to choose.

> GLORIA
> I suppose so. It's just so nice
> spending time with someone who
> shares one's interests. Well, I
> don't have to tell you.

> JUSTIN
> Sorry, I'm not following.

(CONTINUED)

                         GLORIA
               Tessa and Arnold Bluhm.
                    (beat)
               They have so much in common.

          Justin looks across to where Tessa and Sandy are in
          conversation on a bench.

                         JUSTIN
               I think I'd better get Tessa home.
               She gets very tired these days.

                         GLORIA
                    (touching her stomach)
               I wish Sandy was as protective of
               me.

                         JUSTIN
               You've some way to go yet.

          CLOSER ANGLE ON SANDY AND TESSA.

                         SANDY
                    (not looking at her)
               I'm finding it difficult to keep my
               hands off you.

                         TESSA
               Sandy, I'm the size of a house.
               This time next week I'll be in
               hospital having my baby.

                         SANDY
               Can I come and see you?

                         TESSA
                    (a laugh)
               In Uhuru?

                         SANDY
               Christ, you're not having it there!

                         TESSA
               Why not? The Kibera women drop
               their babies there every day. You
               could book Gloria in.

                         SANDY
               It's you I care about.

                         TESSA
               Yes, I know.

CONTINUED: (2)

Tessa pats his hand, stands and crosses to where Justin is
ready to leave.

10   INT. THE QUAYLES' HOUSE - BEDROOM/BATHROOM. NIGHT   10

ANGLE THROUGH OPEN BATHROOM DOOR

Tessa is luxuriating in a blue bubble bath, her pregnant
stomach protruding like a pink island, her eyes closed.

REVEAL JUSTIN

hidden from view, playfully recording her through the doorway
on a small Webcam. The image is appearing simultaneously on a
computer on a desk in the bedroom.

Tessa opens her eyes, sees him in the mirror...and
immediately dips her exposed body under the water.

                    TESSA
                (teasingly)
          Voyeur. Pervert.

                    JUSTIN
          For the brochure. The lovely Isle
          of Tessa, set in a foamy sea.

Tessa throws a sponge at him. He ducks behind the door,
laughing.

                    TESSA
          Don't, Justin. Wipe it, please.

                    JUSTIN
          Ah. I'm not sure my computer skills
          will run to that.

But he resumes his seat at the computer and, smiling still,
erases the image from the screen.

A PING announces incoming e-mail.

                    TESSA
                (calling)
          See who it's from, darling.

MIRROR SHOT - TESSA'S REFLECTION

as she climbs out of the bath, pats herself dry and starts to
put on her underwear.

Justin clicks on the message. The sender isn't identified,
but the message originates from the High Commission's
communal e-mail address.

                                                        (CONTINUED)

It reads: **"What were you and Arnold Bluhm doing in the
Nairobi Hilton Sunday night? Does Justin know?"**

Justin stares at it a moment, then deletes the message as
Tessa enters from the bathroom, still in her underwear.

> TESSA (CONT'D)
> What was it?

> JUSTIN
> Hm?

> TESSA
> The e-mail.

> JUSTIN
> Oh...junk. Some ad.

> TESSA
> For?

> JUSTIN
> The Nairobi Hilton.

He waits for a response. There isn't one.

> JUSTIN (CONT'D)
> Weekend package deal. Two nights
> for the price of one.

She indicates her pregnant abdomen...

> TESSA
> Two guests for the price of one.

...and exits to the landing.

Justin closes his screen, no longer in the mood to write. On
Tessa's Desktop we now see a variety of folders, among them:
"HOUSEHOLD"; "KIBERA"; "AFRICAN WOMEN'S FOUNDATION"; "HAM";
"ARNOLD'S LINKS"; "GRACE MAKANGA".

A moment, then Justin clicks on "ARNOLD'S LINKS". Receives
the prompt: "ENTER PASSWORD". He tries to access "KIBERA".
Same result. He stands and leaves the room.

TRACK WITH JUSTIN next door, into a room set up as a nursery
in anticipation of the birth: an animal frieze around the
walls. Tessa is preparing to hang the Kibera children's
mobile over a baby's cot.

Handing Justin the mobile, she pulls a chair over for him to
stand on.

                    TESSA (CONT'D)
       Make yourself useful.

Justin climbs on the chair and dutifully hangs the mobile
from the lampshade.

                    JUSTIN
       What do you think?

                    TESSA
        (squinting at the mobile)
       It's crooked.

                    JUSTIN
       About a weekend at the Hilton.

                    TESSA
       Bit flashy for my taste.

                    JUSTIN
       Is it? I've never been there.

                    TESSA
       I was there the other night.
       Meeting someone. With Arnold.

She explains no further. He doesn't press. Just straightens
the mobile.

                    JUSTIN
       It was just a thought.

As he steps down off the chair she plants a kiss on his face.

                    TESSA
       Lovely thought. Wrong time, wrong
       venue. Maybe after Arturo is born.

                    JUSTIN
       Tessa, we are not calling him
       Arturo. Or Giuseppe, or Guido.

                    TESSA
        (wicked smile)
       Traditional Manzini names.

                    JUSTIN
       He'll be a quarter Manzini, a
       quarter Prior and half Quayle.

                    TESSA
       Garth, then. My father's name.

>   JUSTIN
>   Absolutely not Garth. Ditto Che.

>   TESSA
>   Che?

>   JUSTIN
>   (playful)
>   Your revolutionary half.

>   TESSA
>   (playful too)
>   Che Muffin Quayle.

>   JUSTIN
>   Muffin!

>   TESSA
>   The Quayle genes. High tea by the
>   jolly old study fire while the
>   starving mob burns London.

Justin smiles.

>   JUSTIN
>   Is that how you see me?

>   TESSA
>   (fondly)
>   No, I see you buying the mob fish
>   and chips while you wait for law
>   and order to return. And I love you
>   the way you are.

Justin smiles. They kiss again. As he turns to go out-

>   TESSA (CONT'D)
>   What about "Arnold"?

He turns.

>   JUSTIN
>   What about Arnold?

>   TESSA
>   As a name. It would a nice gesture.

A beat, then:

>   JUSTIN
>   Perhaps it'll be a girl.
>   (exits)

11   *COMPUTER INSERT A - DOCUMENTARY FOOTAGE*   11

Though these images are unframed and without context, they
will suggest qualitatively that what we're seeing is video
footage from a website. This will be a segment of documentary
about comparative drug prices in Africa and the developed
world: generics as opposed to branded drugs; costs relative
to annual per capita income etc.

12   *EXT./INT. KIBERA - TEMPORARY CLINIC. MORNING*   12

Tessa and Bluhm are on the upper-floor of the only two-storey
building in Kibera, today being used as a training centre.
Bluhm is helping a MIDDLE-AGED AFRICAN WOMAN instruct a group
of YOUNG GIRLS in the principles of midwifery and neonatal
care: plastic dolls with plastic umbilical cords illustrating
the lesson. A poster on the wall advertises a forthcoming pan-
Kenyan tour: Grace Makanga's "Women for Life Crusade". Grace
Makanga is pictured in traditional African dress: a tall,
stately Kenyan woman in her forties.

ANGLE ON TESSA - still heavily pregnant, looking out from the
balcony.

TESSA'S POV

The entire sprawl of the slum is spread out below her: tens
of thousands of shanty huts and the teeming life they house.

In the near distance a queue has formed by a mobile clinical
testing centre - a pale blue Toyota Landcruiser.

Among those in line we pick out JOMO, who, like several other
patients, has in his hand a small jar containing a sample of
his sputum.

REVERSE ANGLE - TESSA, looking towards the Landcruiser. Bluhm
appears at her side.

                    TESSA
          What Kibera needs is a proper
          clinic. A permanent one.

                    BLUHM
          Add it to the wish list.

                    TESSA
          Good. Jomo's getting his HIV test.

                    BLUHM
          Of course. You told him to.

                    TESSA
          It wasn't an order.

                                              (CONTINUED)

12   CONTINUED: 12

                         BLUHM
                    (smiles)
               Wasn't it?

                         TESSA
               What's in those little jars they're
               carrying?

                         BLUHM
               Sputum.

                         TESSA
               That isn't how you test for HIV
               here, is it?

Bluhm follows her gaze to the mobile clinic.

                         BLUHM
               They're testing for TB.
                    (off her enquiring look)
               A small extra service to humanity.

                         TESSA
               Funny thing. Whenever I hear a drug
               company claim "humanity" I want to
               vomit.

                         BLUHM
               They go together. TB and AIDS. Like
               rats and garbage. It makes sense to
               test for it.

But something about Bluhm's manner suggests to Tessa that
there's more to this, something he isn't voicing.

                         TESSA
                    (probing)
               But that isn't why they're doing
               it, is it?

13   *EXT. THE WOODROWS' HOUSE - TERRACE. DAY*   13

The Woodrows are seated at breakfast on the terrace. Seven-
year-old HARRY is kicking a ball and his father, to Gloria's
annoyance, is compliantly kicking it back between spoonfuls.

                         GLORIA
               Sandy, stop encouraging him.
                    (to Harry)
               If you have to do that, do it
               somewhere else.

                                              (CONTINUED)

                              SANDY
                    Oh, he's all right.
                         (to Harry)
                    Go and practise your ball control,
                    Harry.

The boy scowls at his mother and runs off to practise
headers.

                              GLORIA
                    You got in late last night. Did
                    Bernard get away all right?

                              SANDY
                    He had to take the last flight.
                    Went without his dinner. Look out
                    Addis Ababa.

                              GLORIA
                    Did he say anything?

                              SANDY
                    He banged on a bit.

                              GLORIA
                    About?

                              SANDY
                    Traditional British virtues.
                    Terribly overrated, apparently.
                         (as Pellegrin)
                    "Can we afford them in a harsh
                    commercial world, Sandy?"

                              GLORIA
                    I hope you said we couldn't. It's
                    code for "new men wanted".

                              SANDY
                    As long as Porter Coleridge is Head
                    of Mission nobody's going to move
                    up.

                              GLORIA
                    As long as Sir Bernard Pellegrin is
                    Head of Africa Desk, you have a
                    chance.

                              SANDY
                    Oh, I don't know. Anyway there'll
                    be the usual cull of dead wood.
                    Wouldn't be surprised if old Justin
                    went.

                                              (CONTINUED)

13   CONTINUED: (2)   13

                    GLORIA
               (swivels, horrified)
          Justin! Justin's a sweetie!
          It's that bloody bitch! Blighting
          his career with her vile behaviour.

                    SANDY
          I expect the baby'll keep her out
          of trouble.

                    GLORIA
          Think so? Probably as well she's
          having it in the government
          hospital.
               (a beat)
          Considering what colour it's likely
          to be.

CLOSE ANGLE ON TESSA BREAST-FEEDING A BLACK BABY

                              WIDEN TO:

14   INT. UHURU HOSPITAL WARD. DAY   14

A long ward, beds without sheets and pillows; beside each bed
an unplaned pot cupboard fashioned from a packing crate.
Unopened skylights. An unemptied bed-pan in a corner, flies
buzzing around it; others busy at a pile of bloody rags.

Tessa is in the middle bed of one wall. Her face is haggard,
her eyes - shadowed with sleeplessness and pain - reflecting
a profound sadness. Naked to her waist, which is covered in a
kanga cloth, she cradles the NEW-BORN BLACK INFANT to her
left breast, feeding it, her right breast exposed and
waiting.

ANGLE TO REVEAL BLUHM - sitting beside her on a safari cot
with a rumpled blanket...

...AND JUSTIN perched on a cane chair on the other side. An
open notebook, crammed with Tessa's jottings, lies on the
bedside crate, a pen beside it.

15   INT. HOSPITAL CORRIDOR. DAY   15

Carrying a small gift basket of fruit, Sandy is making his
way towards the ward, past a clutter of broken-down trolleys
laden with RECUMBENT PATIENTS: some unconscious, others
reaching out in their pain. He enters Tessa's ward...

16   **INT. WARD. DAY**   16

...and REACTS, visibly taken aback by Tessa's haggard
appearance, her exposed breast, the black baby she's nursing;
and by the presence of both Bluhm and Justin.

                    TESSA
               (a weak smile)
          Hello, Sandy. Thanks for coming.

Bluhm nods to Sandy. Justin stands to shake his hand.

                    SANDY
          I'm so sorry, Tessa. Gloria sends
          her sympathies. What can one say?

He sets down his gift of fruit on the table.

                    TESSA
          It was a boy - did Justin tell you?

                    JUSTIN
          Tessa...

                    TESSA
          This one was born alive, though.
               (to baby)
          Weren't you, my beautiful darling?
               (to Sandy)
          His name is Baraka. It means
          blessing.

                    SANDY
          I don't quite see...

                    TESSA
               (weak smile)
          Who his mother is?

ANGLE TO REVEAL WANZA KILULU

a 15 year-old Kenyan girl-woman in the bed opposite.

Her skinny 12 year-old brother, KIOKO, crouches between her
cupboard and an empty baby cot, fanning his sister's sweating
face with a piece of card torn from a carton. There's an
image on the cardboard: two (*sic*) small yellow-and-black bees
flying in horizontal V-formation against a blue background.
Black lettering close to the torn-off right-hand edge
reads:"48 AMP"; overprinted in red with the word "NOT". As
the makeshift fan moves slowly up and down in Kioko's hand it
gives the little bees the illusion of hovering.

(CONTINUED)

> TESSA (CONT'D)
> Her name's Wanza Kilulu. She's
> fifteen and she's dying. Kioko's
> twelve. He walked forty kilometres
> to keep the flies off his sister
> and her baby. Perhaps that's the
> blessing.

> BLUHM
> The blessing is the child was born
> healthy.

> TESSA
> Yes, Arnold. A healthy orphan with
> a 47-year life expectancy. His
> mother won't last 47 hours.

Sandy looks helplessly at Justin.

> JUSTIN
> Darling, please don't.

> TESSA
> But then they're only Africans.

Sandy looks around for somewhere to sit, finally perches
uncomfortably on the hard frame of the bed.

> BLUHM
> Please sit here, Mr Woodrow. I'll
> wait outside.

He goes out. Sandy remains where he is.

At this point Kioko comes over and gestures to be given the
baby. Tessa hands Baraka to him, then, with a glance at Sandy
daring him to challenge the act, gives the boy Sandy's basket
of fruit. Kioko smiles his thanks. He returns the baby to its
cot. During this:

> SANDY
> What's the...er, camp bed for?

> JUSTIN
> We've been taking turns at night.
> Arnold and myself. Staying with
> Tessa.

> SANDY
> Ah. Yes. I see.

> TESSA
> Poor Sandy. It's all so shocking
> for you, isn't it?

                         SANDY
               No no, not at all.

                         TESSA
                    (to Justin)
               Darling, do you think you could get
               me a fresh bottle of water?

                         SANDY
                    (rising)
               Let me.

                         TESSA
               Justin knows where to get it.

                         JUSTIN
               Back in a minute.
                    (exits)

The moment he's gone, Tessa takes Sandy's hand in hers.

                         TESSA
               He'll be four minutes. Sandy, if I
               tell you something, will you
               listen?

                         SANDY
               God, Tessa...not here.

                         TESSA
               If I told you that poor girl over
               there was being murdered would you
               believe me?

                         SANDY
               Tessa, you're tired, you're
               feverish-

                         TESSA
               We haven't enough evidence yet, but
               when we get it - if I bring it to
               you - will you actually do
               something for once?

                         SANDY
               What you need is rest.

                         TESSA
                    (fiercely)
               Listen to me! Are you listening?

                         SANDY
               Like a hawk.

                                              (CONTINUED)

>   TESSA
>   I'm talking about coincidences.
>   Busy busy busy coincidences in
>   white coats.

>   SANDY
>   Tessa, you've got to stop involving
>   yourself in matters that don't
>   concern you. You're embarrassing
>   the High Commission-

>   TESSA
>   Sod the High Commission.

>   SANDY
>   Me, then. And you're not doing
>   Justin's career any good.

>   TESSA
>   Justin doesn't know what I do.

>   SANDY
>   That doesn't surprise me.

>   TESSA
>   Promise you'll act on what we tell
>   you or I won't let you out of here.

>   SANDY
>   "We?"

>   TESSA
>   Arnold and me.

>   SANDY
>   All right, Tessa, I promise -
>   within reason.

>   TESSA
>   He promises - within reason. Well
>   there's a man.

17   **INT. HOSPITAL CORRIDOR. DAY**   17

Sandy comes out and finds Bluhm in the hellish hallway,
mopping the forehead of a groaning YOUTH on a trolley. Justin
is returning with the water for Tessa.

>   SANDY
>   (to Justin)
>   She's raving, man. You've got to
>   get her to a proper clinic.

17   CONTINUED: 17

> BLUHM
> White doctors, Mr Woodrow?

> SANDY
> Justin, she's your wife, for God's
> sake!

> JUSTIN
> Yes. She's my wife.

> SANDY
> No wonder you two are sharing a
> bloody bed.
>   (exits angrily)

18   **INT. UHURU HOSPITAL WARD. EVENING**   18

TESSA'S POV - A YOUNG MAN IN A WHITE COAT

as he lifts BARAKA from his cot, deposits him into KIOKO's
arms, then briskly steers boy and baby towards the door.

REVEAL TESSA

dressed, her bag packed, ready to leave. Justin is with her.
They're watching this from the far side of the room.

There are three or four WHITE-COATED STUDENTS gathered around
Wanza's bed. Wanza lies motionless, eyes closed, while the
group's leader - a burly, blond-haired man of about forty
(MARKUS LORBEER) - examines her. To judge from his unkempt
appearance, he's been called out in a hurry. He shakes his
head.

WIDEN TO INCLUDE BLUHM, who has crossed to speak to Lorbeer.

TESSA'S POV: BLUHM AND LORBEER

Though inaudible to her and Justin, their conversation is
plainly adversarial. Bluhm seems to be reproaching Lorbeer;
Lorbeer's attitude is defensive.

Eventually Bluhm leans over to confirm what he suspects. He
pulls back Wanza's eyelids, feels for a pulse, then steps
back, having satisfied himself that she is dead. He points
angrily at the corpse, prods Lorbeer accusingly in the chest.

Justin has seen the angry confrontation but is more concerned
about Tessa's distressed reaction. He puts his arms
comfortingly around her. Burying her face in Justin's chest,
Tessa clings to him, weeping uncontrollably.

(CONTINUED)

Across the room Lorbeer has opened Wanza's cupboard and is now scooping into a bag what we assume to be her medicines: small blue boxes marked with a logo we can't clearly see.

Brushing aside the still-protesting Bluhm, Lorbeer leads his assistants from the ward.

ON JUSTIN - half-turned to watch them leave.

ON LORBEER - glancing past Justin at Tessa on his way out.

ON TESSA - staring icily back at him, tears coursing down her face. Bluhm has returned to Tessa's side and, at a gesture from Justin, takes over the comforting.

> JUSTIN
> I'll bring the car round.

19   **EXT. UHURU HOSPITAL/JUSTIN'S CAR. EVENING**   19

Stalls clutter the entrance: VENDORS selling food, drink, tinware, cheap clothing, fake tribal bric-a-brac etc.

Through this tangle Justin's car can be seen making its way with maddening slowness. Nobody is in a hurry to step aside and Justin doesn't use his horn. So it's a yard or two of progress, stop, wait for someone to move; then another yard, another stop, another wait...

20   **INT. CAR (TRAVELLING). NIGHT**   20

Justin is on the road now, taking Tessa home. They're about to pass a small pedestrian group-

REVEALED AS KIOKO AND HIS MOTHER (31), the latter carrying BARAKA in a sling. Making their way back to Miluri.

> TESSA
> Stop the car.

> JUSTIN
> (slowing automatically)
> Tessa-

> TESSA
> It's forty kilometres to Miluri.
> It'll take them all night.

> JUSTIN
> Tessa, we can't...involve ourselves
> in their lives...

> TESSA
> Why?

CONTINUED:

>   JUSTIN
>   Be reasonable. There are millions
>   of people - they all need help.
>   It's what the agencies are for-

>   TESSA
>   These are just three people <u>we</u> can
>   help.

>   JUSTIN
>   I'm sorry, Tessa. I have to put you
>   first. It's you I need to get home.

The car swishes past, leaving the small family behind. Too
exhausted - physically and emotionally - to argue the point,
Tessa says nothing but turns in her seat to look back.

KIOKO'S POV as the car dwindles, Tessa visible through the
rear window, looking back, her hand half raised in a hopeless
gesture of regret and apology.

21   **EXT. THE QUAYLES' HOUSE. DAY**   21

Wearing his straw gardening hat, Justin is showing MUSTAFA
the houseboy how to use pesticide on the flower beds: so much
water into the spray can, add so much powder, swish the
mixture around, then spray - like so.

The powder is in a cardboard carton labelled "TOXIPEST", a
product of the House of ThreeBees: a pale blue box bearing
the logo of three hovering black-and-yellow bees.

>   JUSTIN
>   I think you've enough there now.
>   (a smile)
>   Just the flowers this time, please,
>   Mustafa. Let's not protect the
>   weeds.

>   MUSTAFA
>   The pests must eat too, *bwana*.
>   (laughs)
>   They can eat the weeds.

>   JUSTIN
>   If only they would.

He picks up the "TOXIPEST" and crosses to the verandah.

REVEAL TESSA AND BLUHM seated on the verandah, in earnest
discussion over tea.

As Justin climbs the steps Tessa, her back to him and unaware
of his proximity, continues talking earnestly to Bluhm.

(CONTINUED)

21   CONTINUED: 21

> TESSA
> It's a marriage of convenience,
> Arnold. All it produces is dead
> offspring-

Catching Bluhm's warning look, she breaks off and swings
round in her chair...

...to find Justin only a yard or two behind her, the
""TOXIPEST"" box in his hand.

The expression on Tessa's face - initially shock at being
overheard - alters into a look of such disgust and loathing
that it sears Justin's heart.

> JUSTIN
> Sorry... Didn't mean to interrupt.

Tessa points a quivering finger at the box in Justin's hand.

> TESSA
> (cold white rage)
> What the fuck is that?

> JUSTIN
> (taken aback)
> Pesticide. I don't really approve
> but I told Gloria I'd-

With sudden violence Tessa swipes the box from Justin's hand,
scattering powder across the verandah.

> TESSA
> Get that thing out of my sight!

Bluhm reaches out to calm her, but she's beyond calming. She
thrusts his hand away and burns her glare into Justin's eyes.

> JUSTIN
> If you feel that strongly about it.

He meets Bluhm's eye. Bluhm shrugs as Tessa runs tearfully
into the house.

> JUSTIN (CONT'D)
> It would help if I knew what's
> upsetting her.
> (gestures with the box)
> I mean...this doesn't kill people.
> Unless they swallow it.
> (a beat)
> Does it?

21   CONTINUED: (2)   21

                         BLUHM
                    (a smile)
          No.

                         JUSTIN
          What, then? Why is she
          so...(angry)?

He leaves the thought uncompleted.

                         BLUHM
          You have to trust her, Justin.

                         JUSTIN
          Does she blame me for losing the
          baby?

                         BLUHM
          Of course not. Give her time. Tell
          her I'll be back later.

He starts down the steps. Watched all the way by Justin, he
exits via the garden gate.

22   **COMPUTER INSERT B - DOCUMENTARY FOOTAGE**   22

As before, it will not be apparent that this is a documentary
extract from a website. The topic on this occasion: corrupt
doctors, drug endorsements for sale.

23   **INT. QUAYLES' HOUSE - DRAWING ROOM/BEDROOM. NIGHT**   23

A brick fireplace, handwoven rugs, African masks and shields,
a shelf unit containing books and bound reports; but also a
Madonna and Child by a minor Renaissance Italian master, an
18th-century water colour of the Manzini mansion on Elba and
some antique European pieces, including an Italian inlaid
table. Enough to make Sotheby's drool.

Justin is sitting alone in the dark by an open window (insect-
netted), watching a VIOLENT THUNDERSTORM raging over Nairobi:
sheet lightning illuminating the sky, an almost solid curtain
of rain sweeping across the garden.

We HEAR A CAR outside, see its HEADLIGHTS briefly reflecting
off the rain. A car door slams. The car drives off. Moments
later the HOUSE DOOR IS HEARD CLOSING.

A drenched Tessa enters. She has in her hand the notebook we
saw at Uhuru. She looks exhausted. Switching on the light,
she is momentarily startled to find Justin in the room.

                         TESSA
          You shouldn't have waited up.

                                                      (CONTINUED)

                         JUSTIN
            I've hardly seen you since you left
            hospital.
                 (a beat)
            Was that Arnold's car?

She nods, then crosses to him and kisses him on the mouth.

                         TESSA
            Have you eaten?
                 (off his nod)
            Good. Then go to bed.

She touches his face tenderly.

                         TESSA (CONT'D)
            I'm safe home now.

                         JUSTIN
            You're drenched. Get those wet
            things off and come to bed.

Tessa shakes her head.

                         TESSA
            Something I have to do first. It's
            important.

He takes her hand and holds on to it.

                         JUSTIN
            Tessa, whatever it is you and
            Arnold are doing...I'd like you to
            stop.

                         TESSA
            Who have you been talking to?

                         JUSTIN
            These are my concerns, darling. I'm
            thinking of your health.

                         TESSA
            They've asked you to rein me in.
            And you're doing it.

She goes into the bedroom. Justin follows. Tessa begins to
exchange her wet clothes for dry ones.

                         JUSTIN
            I'd hope you know me better than
            that. Your life is your own. That
            was always our agreement.

23   CONTINUED: (2)   23

                         TESSA
           We agreed my work would be my own.
           That's what makes me who I am. If
           you keep me from doing it who will
           I be?

Suddenly she leans into him, putting her arms around him. He
holds her close.

                         TESSA (CONT'D)
           God, I'm so tired.

                         JUSTIN
           Tessa...please come to bed.

Gathering her resolve, she kisses him, then stands back.
Ready to go on now.

                         TESSA
           Get me up for breakfast.

As she goes out a jolt of THUNDER shakes the house.

24   *INT. QUAYLES' HOUSE - LATER THAT NIGHT.*   24

Tessa, intent on typing a report, unaware of...

...JUSTIN watching her with concern through the open door.

25   *EXT. THE WOODROWS' GARDEN. DAY*   25

This time it's Tessa who is watching Justin. He has come to
advise Gloria about her garden and Tessa, with motives of her
own, has come along with him.

ANGLE ON JUSTIN AND GLORIA

Heads together, examining a bushy plant. Justin fingering its
blossoms. Harry, the Woodrows' young son, can be seen
loitering nearby, dressed in cricket whites, impatient to be
off to his match.

ANGLE ON TESSA

For a few moments she stands watching Justin and Gloria. Then
suddenly, without a word, she turns and heads towards the
house.

26   *INT. SANDY'S HOUSE - OFFICE. DAY*   26

Sandy is taping the handle of Harry's (junior) cricket bat,
trimming the vinyl tape with his desk scissors, overlapping
it carefully around the handle. The telephone conversation
he's having with Kenny Curtiss is therefore via speakerphone.

                                              (CONTINUED)

Having unwound a length of tape, Sandy now clenches the end
between his teeth as he reaches for the scissors.

                    SANDY
               (between clenched teeth)
          Kenny, I can't discuss this on the
          phone-

                    KENNY
          That cow of yours won't give me an
          appointment. You buggers couldn't
          get your tongues far enough up my
          bum two weeks ago. What's changed?

The door opens softly behind Sandy. Tessa enters.

                    SANDY
               (to phone)
          Come to the office. I've got to go
          now.

He disconnects.

                    TESSA
          Trouble with ThreeBees, Sandy?

Sandy puts down the bat and the tape. Unlike Kenny, Tessa
gets his complete attention.

                    SANDY
          Kenny being Kenny.

                    TESSA
          Was that anything to do with my
          report?

                    SANDY
          He's just ranting.

                    TESSA
          You promised you'd do something.

Sandy gets out of his chair and crosses to her. Puts a
placatory hand on her shoulder.

                    SANDY
          I sent your report to London.

                    TESSA
          To Pellegrin?

                    SANDY
          Yes.

                                        (CONTINUED)

                              TESSA
                    And?

                              SANDY
                    There was no official reply.

                              TESSA
                    But there was something, yes?

                              SANDY
                    Just a personal letter.

                              TESSA
                    Saying what?

                              SANDY
                    Nothing I could possibly share with
                    you -

                              TESSA
                    Let me read it.

                              SANDY
                    Out of the question. It's private
                    and extremely compromising. You'll
                    have to take my word.

                              TESSA
                    Not good enough.

          She picks up the 'phone.

                              TESSA (CONT'D)
                    I'll call him myself, then.

                              SANDY
                    No, don't do that. It's serious,
                    Tessa.
                         (pause; off her reaction)
                    I've been told to keep an eye on
                    you.

                              TESSA
                    What??

                              SANDY
                    Trust me, Tessa. This is something
                    it isn't safe for you to pursue.

          He starts to caress her neck.

                              SANDY (CONT'D)
                    I say that as a friend who cares
                    deeply for you-

He starts guiltily as Gloria suddenly appears in the doorway.

> GLORIA
> (to Tessa)
> Oh there you are, Tessa. Your
> husband's waiting for you in the
> car.

Her eye takes in the unfinished cricket bat on the desk.

> GLORIA (CONT'D)
> Harry's match starts in half an
> hour. We need to leave now. Of
> course, if you're too busy ...

> SANDY
> I'll be with you in a sec.

He returns to the desk, busily starts to wind more tape
around the bat's handle.

With a smile at Tessa that could freeze the tropics, Gloria
goes out.

A pause, then:

> TESSA
> What do think of me, Sandy?

> SANDY
> God, Tessa, you're the most
> exciting...(trails off).

> TESSA
> Do you want me?

> SANDY
> God, yes.

> TESSA
> (playing it as a joke)
> You can have me if you show me that
> letter.

He looks at her , uncertain of her intentions.

> SANDY
> Are you serious?

> TESSA
> Why not? Sight of that letter ...
> for me.

> SANDY
>> When?

> TESSA
>> When I get back from Loki.

The impatient BEEPING of a car horn is heard from outside.

Sandy picks up the cricket bat and stands to go.

> TESSA (CONT'D)
>> No, Sandy, you have to show me the
>> letter now. That's the deal.

Sandy closes his eyes. A long moment.

Returning to the desk he unlocks a drawer, takes out a
handwritten letter on expensive creamy paper. He lays it on
the desk. Then:

> SANDY
>> If anyone ever found out I'd shown
>> you that, I'd be ruined. Read it
>> once, put it back in the drawer. Do
>> you promise?

> TESSA
>> I promise.

He steals a brief kiss from Tessa's unresisting mouth and
then leaves.

CU THE LETTER

CU THE SAME LETTER on another desktop

> PANNING TO:

A COMPUTER SCREEN

showing more of the grainy images we've so far been seeing
unidentified. This one the Grace Makanga website.

There's video footage of GRACE MAKANGA addressing the World
Health Organization; a brief biography of G.M.; and below,
under the heading: "WOMEN FOR LIFE CRUSADE", a map of Kenya
showing the itinerary, with dates, of G.M.'s proposed tour of
lectures and conferences.

We see that it starts in Mombasa after Christmas, travels
west and north to Lodwar and Loki during January, then turns
south and east, around the southern tip of Lake Turkana to
Marsabit, before returning to Nairobi early in March.

27   *INT. TESSA'S DEN. NIGHT*   27

TESSA at her computer. REVEALING that this has been the
source of the unidentified documentaries. Her research. Her
work.

The purloined letter is on the desk beside her.

She is typing the e-mail to Ham that we will later hear in
full.

27A   *INT. HIGH COMMISSION - SANDY'S OFFICE. DAY*   27A

The door flies open and a raging KENNY CURTISS bursts in.
Miriam behind him, gestures apologetically at Sandy. Couldn't
keep him out.

                    CURTISS
          You buggers got me into this
          fucking thing. It's bleeding me
          dry. Leeching my other divisions.
          The Bank's starting to cut up rough-

                    SANDY
          That's something you'll have to
          take up with Porter.

                    CURTISS
          That useless prick? Don't make me
          laugh, I'll get hiccups.

                    SANDY
          London, then. Wherever.

                    CURTISS
          Vancouver? Basel? Done that.
          Vancouver says talk to Basel, Basel
          says talk to London. "London's been
          here," I said. "Guzzling my fucking
          champagne."

                    SANDY
          We'll go and see Porter together.

                    CURTISS
          When?

                    SANDY
          Now. Give me a minute.

                    CURTISS
          Sixty seconds. I'm counting.

EXT. AIRCRAFT HANGAR. DAY

Justin's car pulls up outside a hangar in a field. There's an elderly prop aircraft on the hardstand, being prepped for flight.

Justin climbs out of the car and goes around first to open the front passenger door for Tessa, then to the boot to remove her bag. He finds Bluhm already doing it.

> JUSTIN
> (taking bag from him)
> Thank you, Arnold. I can manage
> that.
> (to them both)
> I still don't see why you couldn't
> wait a few weeks. Why go all the
> way up to Loki?

Tessa exchanges a flicker of a glance with Bluhm.

> TESSA
> We want to hear Grace Makanga
> speak. She won't be in Nairobi,
> will she, Arnold?

> BLUHM
> No, she's going to New York at the
> end of the month.

JUSTIN - a reluctant sigh of acceptance.

> TESSA
> (to Justin)
> Don't wait to see us off, darling.
> It could be ages yet.

> JUSTIN
> Well, if you're sure....

> TESSA
> (kissing him; teasingly)
> Too hot to be standing around.

He wraps his arms around her. She hugs him back, burying her face in his chest, lingering over the parting.

Justin stands watching as the two of them head towards the plane, Bluhm taking her luggage from her. Tessa turns to blow a last kiss.

> JUSTIN
> See you in a week, then.

(CONTINUED)

28   CONTINUED: 28

She waves. Then is gone.

JUSTIN'S POV: AN ACACIA TORTILLA

29   **EXT. THE WOODROWS' HOUSE. DAWN**   29

A SLOW TRAVELLING SHOT takes us through the crash gates, past
the wire-topped security fence and across the neat lawns of a
large stone house with leaded mock-Tudor windows in the smart
hilltop suburb favoured by Nairobi's diplomats.

From the house we hear a TELEPHONE RINGING, growing louder as
we approach. At that hour when a phone call stops the heart.

                    SANDY'S VOICE
          Woodrow. Are they sure? Tell no-
          one. Do nothing till I get there.

Sound of receiver being replaced.

                    GLORIA'S VOICE
          What's happened?

No reply.

31   **EXT. LAKE TURKANA. DAWN**   31

Here at the southern tip of Lake Turkana a mist hangs low
over the unrippled waters. Nothing moves on the lake; no
wildlife is visible, not even a bird. The reason...

A POLICE LAND ROVER, parked behind an overturned four-track;
the four-track lying on its side, doors closed, one window
slightly open. TWO COVERED BODIES are being loaded into the
back of the police vehicle by KENYAN CONSTABLES. ONE PLAIN-
CLOTHES KENYAN DETECTIVE is photographing the scene; ANOTHER
is using a pencil to pick up an empty Oshodi beer bottle.

32   **INT. HIGH COMMISSION - SANDY'S OFFICE/CORRIDOR. DAY**   32

Miriam pops her head around the door to where Sandy sits at
his desk, nervously tapping a pencil against his blotter.

                    MIRIAM
          He's here.

Sandy stands up, walks out of his office and heads down the
corridor.

32A   **INT. HIGH COMMISSION - JUSTIN'S OFFICE. DAY**   32A

Perfectly groomed as always, Justin is watering his window
plants. Unaware as yet.

                                              (CONTINUED)

The door opens behind him and Sandy enters. He doesn't come
all the way into the room but closes the door and stands with
his back to it. Justin turns to see who it is.

> JUSTIN
> Hi, Sandy. Caught me skiving, I'm
> afraid. Gloria well?

He returns to watering his plants.

> SANDY
> Gloria's fine.
> (clears his throat)
> You haven't heard from Tessa, I
> suppose?

> JUSTIN
> She's up north with Arnold Bluhm.

> SANDY
> Look, old chap, do you think you
> could stop doing that a moment?

Justin stops watering and turns, alerted by both the request
and its tone.

> JUSTIN
> Something wrong, Sandy?

> SANDY
> Did she say anything about
> returning by road?

> JUSTIN
> From Loki? Wouldn't surprise me,
> knowing Tessa. I hope not. That's
> dangerous...
> (beginning to get it)
> ...country. Sandy, what is this?

> SANDY
> We're getting reports of a white
> woman and a black driver...found
> early this morning, southern end of
> Lake Turkana.
> (pause)
> Dead. Killed, it seems.

Justin does not sag or crumple. His expression hardly
changes. He merely smooths back his hair with his free hand,
then turns again to the window box to continue his task, his
emotions under the tightest of reins.

(CONTINUED)

                        JUSTIN
          And you think it might be Tessa.

                        SANDY
          It's not looking good. Seems they
          hired a car and driver at Loki,
          then headed east. They spent the
          night at Lodwar....
               (a beat)
          They shared a room, Justin.
               (another beat)
          The dead black isn't Bluhm.
               (a beat)
          I'm most terribly sorry.

                        JUSTIN
          How sure are you?

                        SANDY
          It's not looking good, Justin.

CLOSE ANGLE - JUSTIN

as the watertight doors of his emotions close inside him,
containing the pain. This place is not private enough.

                        JUSTIN
          Good of you to tell me, Sandy.
          Can't have been pleasant.

Having completed his watering, he sets down the can.

33   **EXT. MORTUARY. EVENING**   33

In the waiting area outside the mortuary building are JUSTIN,
SANDY and a KENYAN POLICE INSPECTOR. They're watching a body
being unloaded from a truck, carried inside by ATTENDANTS.
Not Tessa, but a reminder of what Tessa may now be, what
they've come to ascertain.

Another MORTUARY ATTENDANT appears from within the building.
Gestures for them to enter.

34   **INT. MORTUARY. EVENING**   34

TRACK WITH THE GROUP OF FOUR along a damp corridor, passing
rooms on either side containing nothing but empty stone
slabs. Only in the last room are there bodies: two per slab,
laid head to toe. The floor is puddled with disinfectant, the
walls wet from spraying.

A DOCTOR is waiting by a slab on which a single body lies,
under a mass of winding sheet. From beneath it protrude two
grotesquely distended human feet.

CONTINUED:

One dead arm dangles over the board's edge, its sausage
fingers coated in congealed black blood, the fingertips an
unnatural aquamarine blue.

The doctor beckons to Justin, who steps forward, Sandy
shadowing him. The doctor rolls back the sheet, revealing the
body beneath. What Justin sees we, mercifully, do not.

JUSTIN'S REACTION

Other than a sharp intake of breath he makes no sound.

> SANDY
> Dear God....

> POLICE INSPECTOR
> (to Justin)
> You know this lady, sir?

> JUSTIN
> (slowly, controlled)
> Yes, I do, thank you. It's my wife.
> Tessa Quayle.

Suddenly Sandy breaks away, barely making it in time to a
cracked handbasin, where he vomits.

Justin crosses to him, and puts a comforting arm around
Sandy's shoulder; as though Sandy, not he, were the bereaved.

35   *EXT. NAIROBI STREET/VAN. DAY*   35

A BLACK VOLKSWAGEN VAN with tinted windows and CD plates is
making its way through heavy city traffic.

It passes a street hoarding: three yellow-and-black bees
flying in arrow formation on a sky-blue ground; the legend:

"THREEBEES BUZZY FOR YOUR HEALTH".

It passes Mustafa walking along the pavement with a FRIEND.
As they pass a barbershop Mustafa's attention is caught by a
television playing inside. A black-and-white TV is showing a
local news item on the murders. The dead African driver
features among library shots of the victims. Bluhm's image
appears last - over it the word *"Missing"*.

37   *INT. THE WOODROWS' KITCHEN. EARLY EVENING*   37

Here, by contrast, Gloria's TV news is from the regional
affiliate of an international channel (CNN, BBC). Here it's
shots of the crime scene, a view of the bedroom at Lodwar
(coyly captioned *"the bedroom at Lodwar"*), then a library shot
of the murdered British diplomat's wife, and finally, an image
of the black doctor *"sought by police"*.

                                                      (CONTINUED)

37   CONTINUED:

ON JOMO, hovering in the kitchen doorway. Trying to watch the
news.

REVEAL GLORIA AND SANDY at the sink: Gloria is sluicing a
carving knife, Sandy drying.

> GLORIA
> Jomo, I've told you twice - we're
> doing it ourselves tonight.

Jomo reluctantly disappears.

> GLORIA (CONT'D)
> Wretched boy.

With a little shudder she passes the carving knife she has
been washing to Sandy for drying. Turning from the sink, she
picks up a small silver box, takes from it a joint, lights
it. She draws deeply on it, then offers a toke to Sandy. He
shakes his head.

> SANDY
> Do you think that's doing the baby
> any good?

> GLORIA
> I'm not inhaling.
>   (irritably)
> Anyway, it helps me relax.

She stubs out the joint.

> SANDY
> It's doing a wonderful job.

> GLORIA
>   (musingly, indicating TV)
> What were they doing wandering
> around in the middle of nowhere?

> SANDY
> They weren't wandering. They were
> on their way home.

> GLORIA
> Loki to Nairobi? Via Turkana?

> SANDY
> I expect they wanted to see the
> lake.

> GLORIA
>   (sarcastic)
> How romantic of them.

(CONTINUED)

Sandy makes no comment.

> GLORIA (CONT'D)
> You said their throats were cut -
> that <u>was</u> the mutilation, wasn't it?
>   (off Sandy's nod)
> Why lock the bodies in the car? If
> I were a bandit I'd leave my
> victims to the jackals.

> SANDY
> I'm sure you would, my dear.

Clearly the cutting of Tessa's throat is a subject Sandy
prefers not to dwell on. He sets the knife down half dried.
Gloria picks it up, inspects it, then takes the dish cloth
from his hand and sets about finishing the job herself.

> GLORIA
> For a soldier's son you're really
> quite squeamish, aren't you, Sandy?
> Has anyone told Justin?

> SANDY
> Told him what?

> GLORIA
> That she was raped first.

> SANDY
> He wanted the details. He was given
> them.

> GLORIA
> I think he's taking it rather well.

> SANDY
> If you mean showing no emotion, I
> agree. Something of a cold fish,
> our house guest.

> GLORIA
> What would you prefer? Girlish
> hysterics?

A polite cough behind them freezes the action.

REVEAL JUSTIN, dressed for outdoors.

> JUSTIN
> Not an inconvenient moment, I hope.

> GLORIA
> (stubs out her roach)
> Perfect timing. Just finished.

> SANDY
> No need for you to go, you know. I
> wish you'd let me do it for you.

> GLORIA
> Yes, let Sandy go, Justin.
> (her most alluring smile)
> Stay here with me.

> JUSTIN
> You're both very kind. This is
> something I have to do myself.

38   **EXT. THE QUAYLES' HOUSE. EARLY EVENING**   38

The PRESS are camped outside in force, and not only the press. A couple of opportunistic VENDORS in Uncle Sam pants and top hats have opened a tea stand; others are cooking maize on a charcoal brazier. Lacklustre POLICEMEN can be seen hanging around a beaten-up patrol car like sluggish flies, yawning and smoking cigarettes.

THE HIGH COMMISSION'S VOLKSWAGEN VAN passes the house and stops. One servant driving; another riding shotgun. In the back: Justin and Sandy.

The pressmen show little interest. Until the van suddenly reverses at speed and swings into the gateway, just as the gates are opened from inside. Before the newsmen have time to crowd through, the van is inside and the gates have shut.

A babble of questions can be heard as the house door opens and Sandy and Justin step inside.

> FIRST JOURNALIST'S VOICE (O.C.)
> Reckon Bluhm topped her?

> SECOND JOURNALIST'S VOICE (O.C.)
> Hey, Justin, my proprietor's
> offering mega-bucks...

39   **INT. THE QUAYLES' HOUSE. EARLY EVENING**   39

Weeping profusely, Mustafa has run to Justin in the darkened hall. Justin draws him close, pats his back comfortingly while an embarrassed Sandy looks away.

ANGLE - OTHER SERVANTS WAITING THEIR TURN IN THE SHADOWS

39   CONTINUED: 39

They include ESMERELDA, a Sudanese teenager. Only Esmerelda
among the servants is not weeping.

The moment Justin releases his hold on Mustafa, Esmerelda
steps forward for attention. Justin clasps both her hands.
She lays her braided forehead against him in silent grief.

                    JUSTIN
                 (to Sandy)
              Tessa's family.

                    SANDY
              Half East Africa's unemployables by
              the look of it.

An ELDERLY WOMAN is next. Justin fondles her cheek.

                    MUSTAFA
                 (to Justin)
              Police came yesterday, *bwana*. They
              took away Mama Tessa's things.

                    SANDY
                 (to Justin)
              Better make a list of what's
              missing. I'll look into it.

With a nod, Justin starts upstairs. Sandy waits until he has
disappeared from view before making for the drawing room.

40   **INT. THE QUAYLES' HOUSE. EARLY EVENING**   40

Sandy looks around, crosses immediately to the inlaid
Italian table, opens the drawer and begins to rummage
inside....

41   **INT. BEDROOM**   41

TESSA'S DESK: drawers wide open, books and excavated box
files strewn over the floor. A clean rectangle on the desk
indicates where Tessa's computer used to be.

42   **INT. DRAWING ROOM**   42

Sandy urgently sifting through the drawer's contents: old
Christmas cards; defunct invitations; a get-well card from
Ghita, a condolence note signed "LOVE, ARNOLD"...

43   **INT. BEDROOM**   43

TESSA'S DRESSING TABLE: cosmetics, creams, lotions - all as
she left them. Justin looks away, crosses to the wardrobe and
opens it.

                                                        (CONTINUED)

ANGLE – WARDROBE: Tessa's clothes still on the rail, her
shoes neatly ranged on the floor.

Not ready to deal with this either, Justin turns his
attention to a pile of bedding stacked lumpily on a shelf
above. Reaching up, he runs his hand behind the bedding,
feels his way along the shelf until he finds a small
LACQUERED JEWEL BOX. He lifts it down, sets it on the bed,
opens it.

Inside are items of jewellery; insurance policies, a will; a
photo of Tessa and Justin taken at their wedding on Elba; a
snapshot of a young woman (BIRGIT) holding the hand of a
blond toddler (KARL)...and a flattened-out cardboard
container bearing the ThreeBees logo. The box is labelled:"12
AMPULES DYPRAXA" and overstamped in red:"NOT FOR RESALE". A
date has been added in Tessa's hand and the words: "WANZA
KILULU".

But Justin's eye is taken by something else: a folded sheet
of blue HM Stationery Office notepaper. He unfolds it. What
Sandy has been seeking, Justin has found.

As Justin scans the text, we hear:

                    SANDY'S VOICE (V.O.)
          Darling Tessa, you have hurt me
          more than you know. Trusting you to
          be honourable, I afforded you,
          against all the rules, an
          opportunity which you have abused
          in the worst way...

44   INT. DRAWING ROOM   44

Sandy desperately ransacking the shelves, pulling down books
and bound reports, among which we see: "FACTORS INFLUENCING
DONOR EFFECTIVENESS IN KENYA-BASED AID AGENCIES", its author
"J. QUAYLE". Justin's claim to usefulness.

                    SANDY'S VOICE (V.O.)
          ...I beg you – for the sake of my
          career – to return what you took.
          If you will not, then at least save
          what is left of me by chucking in
          your ridiculous sham of a marriage –
          as I will mine...

45   INT. BEDROOM   45

Justin finishes reading the letter, his teeth clenched.

45   CONTINUED: 45

                          SANDY'S VOICE (V.O.)
                    ...and bolting with me to the end
                    of the earth. I love you, I love
                    you and I love you. Sandy.

46   **INT. DRAWING ROOM**   46

        Sandy starts guiltily, caught in mid-rummage as Justin
        enters, carrying the lacquered jewel box.

                          JUSTIN
                    Sorry to have been so long, Sandy.

                          SANDY
                    I was...tidying up. They've been in
                    here too. Anything missing
                    upstairs?

                          JUSTIN
                    Her computer. Her disks. All her
                    files. It's quite a shambles.

                          SANDY
                        (indicating box)
                    What's in that?

                          JUSTIN
                    Her will. It seems she wanted to be
                    buried in Africa.

                                            CUT TO:

47   **EXT. KIBERA. DAY**   47

        A LINE OF AFRICAN WOMEN, identically dressed, winding their
        solemn way up the hill from Kibera towards Langata.

48   **EXT. ROAD. DAY**   48

        Kioko on a dusty unmade road, walking towards Langata...

49   **EXT. LANGATA CEMETERY. DAY**   49

        The lush grassy hill of Langata with its ornamental trees and
        below it, in the near distance, the smoky-brown smear of
        Kibera. Here the dead live better than the living.

        Several funerals are taking place simultaneously, as though
        in competition one with another: services in English,
        services in Swahili; burials Christian and non-Christian;
        funerals with song, funerals accompanied by mass prayer.

        TESSA'S GRAVESITE

                                                    (CONTINUED)

Like the bullseye of a target, Tessa's grave is surrounded by concentric horseshoes of mourners and witnesses while a GRIZZLED OLD BLACK PRIEST intones the burial service.

The open grave lies beneath a jacaranda tree beside a smaller grave marked with a temporary wooden cross bearing the name *"Garth Quayle"* and the single date of his birth and death. At its edge JUSTIN and the priest are standing.

The inner horseshoe comprises the High Commission crowd.

Behind them is the AFRICAN WOMEN'S CHOIR - now arriving - and, already there, the servants: ESMERELDA, MUSTAFA, the one-armed UGANDAN BOY, JOMO and several others.

The outermost horseshoe consists of a broken ring of KENYAN POLICEMEN and PHOTO-JOURNALISTS, jockeying with one another for position. With the Kenyan police is a tall, lean white man, later to be identified as DETECTIVE-INSPECTOR DEASEY.

Last of all, behind them and quite alone, is the small figure of KIOKO. He's clutching something to his chest, both spindly arms curled protectively around it.

The priest concludes his prayer. FOUR AFRICAN PALLBEARERS step forward to lift the coffin by its webbing straps. As they commence to lower it the photographers burst past the servants and fire off their camera shots.

Justin swings around to confront them. But before he can address the photographers he's distracted by-

-TWO RAGGED KENYANS trundling a wheelbarrow of wet concrete towards the grave. Its tyre is flat and the concrete is slopping over the sides.

> JUSTIN
> What are they doing? Will someone
> please explain what they're doing?

> GHITA
> It's concrete, Justin. To keep out
> grave robbers.

> JUSTIN
> (angrily)
> Tessa expressed a wish to lie in
> African soil, not in bloody
> concrete. Nothing can grow in
> concrete. Kindly tell them to go,
> please, Ghita.

(CONTINUED)

49   CONTINUED: (2)   49

Ghita relays this to the contractors, who shrug, turn their barrow around and leave. The press seize upon the dismissal as another photo-opportunity.

> JUSTIN (CONT'D)
> (to press photographers)
> You too, please, gentlemen. It was
> kind of you to come. Thank you.

Surprisingly, the journalists pack up and leave like lambs. Never before been asked to fuck off with such politeness.

The lowering of the coffin resumes. And now, for the first time since Tessa's death, we see Justin sag. Ghita and Gloria come immediately to his side and take an arm each.

The Kibera women, having configured themselves as a choir, begin to sing:

> WOMEN'S CHOIR
> *Kwa heri*, Mama Tessa...
> Little Mama, our friend, goodbye...
> You came to us, Mama Tessa,
> You gave us all your heart...
> *Kwa heri*, Tessa, goodbye...
> Goodbye from all our hearts....

As the coffin strikes bottom Justin winces. And again as the first shovel-load of earth clatters hollowly on to its lid.

The High Commission crowd begins to disperse. Though Ghita tries to pull Justin away with them, he stands his ground.

ANGLE ON KIOKO - who has come forward to the graveside. Justin recognises him immediately.

Revealing at last the treasure he has been clutching to his breast, Kioko stoops and lays it upon the grave.

The gift is a fan-shaped segment of cardboard fashioned from a carton: the same piece Kioko used in Uhuru to cool his dying sister's face. On its blank reverse side he has written in felt-tipped capitals: "SLEAP WITH WANZA".

Justin reaches for the boy's hand, but having delivered what he walked eight hours to deliver, Kioko runs off.

Justin bends to look more closely at the plaque. He picks it up. Turns it over.

On the face side we see again the two bees against their pale blue background and, close to the torn right-hand edge, the black lettering: "48 AMP", overprinted with a red "NOT". But now it makes sense.

(CONTINUED)

>   JUSTIN
>   (to himself)
>   Forty-eight ampules Dypraxa. Not
>   for resale.

CU 3-BEES LOGO

                                          WIDENING TO:

50   **_EXT. THE QUAYLES' GARDEN. DAY_**   50

The logo is now on the "TOXIPEST" packet in Justin's hand as
he contemplates it. It prompts a memory.

>   JUSTIN
>   (anguished)
>   "A marriage of convenience." Is
>   that how you saw us?

He raises his eyes and looks in his pain across the garden.

REVEAL TESSA seated on the verandah, her back to him. She
swings around—

—and we REPRISE THE EXPRESSION ON TESSA'S FACE from that
earlier garden scene: shock at finding Justin within earshot,
followed by a look of disgust and loathing: an image burned
indelibly into Justin's psyche, re-created here by him...

>   JUSTIN'S VOICE (V.O.)
>   "Diplomacy, therefore, as we've
>   demonstrated, is the very map and
>   marker of civilization...

51   **_INT. LECTURE HALL - LONDON. DAY_**   51

JUSTIN, two years younger and wearing a dark three-piece suit,
is concluding a dull lecture to a bored audience of
international lawyers.

>   JUSTIN
>   "...pointing nations the safest way
>   through country fraught with
>   peril..."
>   (pause)
>   Sir Bernard Pellegrin has asked me
>   to convey his regrets that he was
>   unable to deliver his lecture in
>   person, and I thank you on my own
>   behalf for your kind attention.

To a scattering of unenthusiastic applause, Justin gathers his
papers together and prepares to leave...

51   CONTINUED:

                    TESSA
          Whose map was Britain using, "Sir
          Bernard", when it ignored the
          United Nations and invaded Iraq?

The audience stirs restlessly.

DISCOVER TESSA ABBOTT

on her feet in the auditorium: pale, waif-like, 22 years old.
Sunlight shafting through the window has all but obliterated
her face, so that it appears as a negative halo: a mass of
light framed by the darkness of her hair, the high choir-boy
collar of her white blouse enhancing the angelic effect.

Squinting, Justin shifts his head the better to see her.

                    TESSA (CONT'D)
          Or is it more "diplomatic" to bend
          to the will of a superpower?

                    JUSTIN
          I can't speak for Sir Bernard-

                    TESSA
          I thought that's why you were here.

                    JUSTIN
            (a smile)
          Diplomats go where they're sent.

                    TESSA
          So do labradors.

                    JUSTIN
          Sir Bernard would no doubt argue
          that when peaceful means are
          exhausted...

JUSTIN'S POV - TESSA

as finally he gets the angle right and brings her into
definition. The beauty of an angel - an angel with a cudgel.

                    TESSA
          Not exhausted, Mr Quayle, just
          lying in the way of the tanks.
            (passionate)
          Why take sixty years to build an
          international organization to avoid
          wars then blow it up because your
          bloody car's running out of petrol?

Groans are coming from the audience. Tessa not knowing when
to stop, as usual.

                    MALE STUDENT
               Sit down, Tessa, for Chrissake.

Justin's heart goes out to her.

                    JUSTIN
               The questioner makes a valid point.
               Whether it is or not, a nation's
               foreign policy should not appear to
               be determined by narrow commercial
               interests...

He has tried to rescue her but she won't be rescued.

                    TESSA
               Then please explain why this
               pathetic country you're paid to
               apologize for burned its diplomatic
               credentials...

Justin tries to interrupt but she rolls over him like a tank.

                    TESSA (CONT'D)
               ...and killed thousands of innocent
               people for a few lousy barrels of
               oil and a photo-opportunity on the
               White House lawn?

She stops, less certain now but still on her feet, braving
the jeers.

The audience has begun to walk out. Row after row is now
emptying around Tessa.

Stepping down from the podium, Justin crosses to where she is
standing, alone and abandoned among the empty seats. What he
aches to do is put his arms comfortingly around her, but
protocol doesn't permit the gesture.

                    JUSTIN
               That took courage.

                    TESSA
                    (shakes her head)
               Anyone can be rude. I'm always
               doing this...I get carried away...

Justin places his hand gently on her shoulder.

She looks up at him; her defiance softened, her underlying
vulnerability disclosed by his kindness.

                                                  (CONTINUED)

51   CONTINUED: (3)

                            TESSA (CONT'D)
                    Thank you for trying to protect me.

52   **EXT. THE QUAYLES' NAIROBI GARDEN. DAY**   52

The verandah chairs are empty. Tessa's ghost has gone.

Another presence makes itself felt at Justin's side as he
emerges from his reverie. Someone gently touches his arm. He
jumps.

REVEAL GHITA

                            GHITA
                    Sorry. You were miles away.

                            JUSTIN
                    Yes. Yes I was.

                            GHITA
                    I got your message. How can I help,
                    Justin? You know I'm here for you.

                            JUSTIN
                    Thank you, Ghita. You're a good
                    friend.

She smiles at him. More than a good friend, perhaps, if he'll
let her be.

                            JUSTIN (CONT'D)
                    I wanted to ask you...rather a
                    delicate question. Perhaps I should
                    say indelicate. Please forgive me
                    for asking it.

                            GHITA
                    No, anything.

                            JUSTIN
                    What were Tessa and Arnold doing at
                    Lake Turkana?

Ghita's face sets. Not the question she was expecting. Not
what she thought he'd summoned her for.

                            GHITA
                    Oh. I see.

                            JUSTIN
                    If you'd rather not say...

> GHITA
> (edge)
> What do you think they were doing?

> JUSTIN
> I don't know.
> (a beat)
> You were Arnold's friend as much as
> Tessa's.

> GHITA
> He didn't kill Tessa, Justin. You
> should be ashamed even to be
> thinking it. He loved her and she
> loved him.

> JUSTIN
> God knows, they spent enough time
> together to give the impression...

He runs his hand through his hair. Can't say the word.

> GHITA
> You know what this place is like.
> If you can't have sex you have
> other people's sex. Real or
> imagined.

A beat, then Ghita opens her handbag and removes her purse.
She rummages inside it until she finds what she wants: a
snapshot. She hands it wordlessly to Justin.

INSERT PHOTO - GHITA WITH BLUHM AND ANOTHER YOUNG MAN

Ghita's arm around Bluhm, Bluhm's arm around the man.

> GHITA (CONT'D)
> Claude. Arnold's boyfriend.

Justin shakes his head. Had no idea. The revelation has
cleared Tessa of one count of adultery at least.

> GHITA (CONT'D)
> It's illegal here. You don't shout
> about it.

> JUSTIN
> She could have told me.

> GHITA
> Perhaps she didn't think you needed
> to know.

                                          CUT TO:

52   CONTINUED: (2)   52

JUSTIN'S CAR, picking its way over an unsurfaced road,
swerving every few yards to avoid a major pot-hole.

53   ***EXT. MILURI VILLAGE. DAY***   53

The car comes to a halt at an improvised road block, set up
on the edge of the village by a GROUP OF EMACIATED BOYS. They
swarm to the car window.

> BOY
> (in Swahili)
> *Good day, bwana. This is a toll*
> *road. You pay to keep up this fine*
> *road. Fifty shillings.*

Justin replies briefly in Swahili as he hands the boy a
banknote through the window. The boy dances away in triumph,
waving the note in the air. The barrier is removed. Justin
drives on. The boys run after the car. Justin smiles.

54   ***EXT. MARKET. DAY***   54

A brief MONTAGE as JUSTIN questions some of the VILLAGERS to
discover where Kioko lives. He's an anomaly here: a lone
white man in a large black settlement.

ANGLE ON A TOYOTA LANDCRUISER IN THREEBEES LIVERY, parked
with its tailgate open. The truck bed loaded with medical
equipment. Mobile clinic.

Carrying baby BARAKA, KIOKO joins a line of MOTHERS AND
CHILDREN which has formed to receive child inoculations. The
NURSES administering the vaccines are black, as is the DOCTOR
supervising.

Here - on foot, having parked his car - Justin finds Kioko.

> JUSTIN
> Hello, Kioko. I've been looking for
> you.

> KIOKO
> Don't want no trouble, *bwana*.

Inside the Landcruiser one of the nurses is making a call on
a mobile phone.

> JUSTIN
> You're not in trouble. I just want
> to talk to you.
> (indicating mobile clinic)
> Is this where Wanza was treated?
> Before she went to hospital?

54   CONTINUED: 54

No answer.

                         NURSE
              Next.

A YOUNG MOTHER, two or three places ahead in the line and
coughing painfully, presents her baby. The attending nurse
holds out her hand for a medical card. There isn't one.

ANGLE - THE NURSE ON THE PHONE in the Landcruiser.

55   **INT. NAIROBI OFFICE. DAY**   55

where a WHITE-COATED EUROPEAN MAN has taken the call. He
hangs up and dials a number...

BACK TO SCENE

Protesting tearfully, the cardless mother is led out of the
line by the nurse, to be replaced by another.

                    JUSTIN
               (to doctor)
          Why was she turned away?

                    DOCTOR
          She refuses treatment.

                    JUSTIN
          She seemed keen enough.

                    DOCTOR
          This woman is a TB patient. She has
          discontinued her treatment. Her
          card was cancelled.

                    JUSTIN
          All the more reason to inoculate
          the child, I'd have thought.

                    DOCTOR
          This is diphtheria vaccine. What is
          your interest, please?

Kioko is tugging fearfully at Justin's sleeve.

                    JUSTIN
          My name is Quayle. I'm from the
          British High Commission.

                    DOCTOR
          Do you see any of your countrymen
          here, Mr Quayle?

56   ***INT. CAR (TRAVELLING). DAY***   56

From behind we see a man (CRICK?) taking the call from the
Nairobi office on his car phone. He nods, disconnects,
dials...

BACK TO SCENE

                          JUSTIN
              Do you have a card, Kioko?

Kioko shows Justin his medical card. Justin examines it.

                          JUSTIN (CONT'D)
              This is in Wanza's name.
                  (indicating card)
              What does "IC" mean?

                          DOCTOR
              Informed Consent. It means she
              consented to treatment. They have
              family medical entitlement.

                          JUSTIN
              What treatment?
                  (off his silence)
              Dypraxa?

                          DOCTOR
              Yes.

                          JUSTIN
              And if they don't consent? They
              lose the right to medical care?

                          DOCTOR
              I do not make the rules.

Before Justin can question him further a police car, summoned
in response to the phone calls, draws up alongside.

Kioko shrinks back in alarm.

                          POLICE DRIVER
              Mr Quayle?

                          JUSTIN
              Yes.

                          POLICE DRIVER
              You will come with us, please.

As Justin climbs into the police car he glances back. Sees-

                                                    (CONTINUED)

56   CONTINUED:

-KIOKO being questioned by a SECOND POLICEMAN.

57   **INT. POLICE STATION. DAY**   57

Justin is sitting on a hard straight-backed chair. One
policeman is leaning against a wall, the other perched on the
edge of a table, tapping a stick against his own knee. To a
Kenyan it would be a threatening gesture.

On the table there's a folded newspaper and an electric fan.
The fan whirs slowly, fluttering the pages of the newspaper,
stirring the air without cooling it.

                    POLICEMAN # 1 (SEATED)
               Why did you come to talk to this
               boy?

                    JUSTIN
               He attended my wife's funeral.
               I came to thank him.

                    POLICEMAN # 2
               You drove forty kilometres for
               this?

                    JUSTIN
               He'd walked it.

                    POLICEMAN # 1
               We know about your wife, Mr Quayle.

He picks up the newspaper, displays it.

There's a photograph of the funeral, two smaller pictures
inset - one of Tessa, one of Bluhm - and the headline:
"BELGIAN DOCTOR SOUGHT IN MURDER OF DIPLOMAT'S WIFE".

                    JUSTIN
               Thank you. I've seen it.

                    POLICEMAN # 1
                    (a smirk)
               He was her lover, this Bluhm?

                    JUSTIN
               So people are pleased to tell me.

                    POLICEMAN # 1
               These men you hired to kill them -
               they rape and kill her, they let
               him go. Where did you find them?

                    JUSTIN
               Perhaps I asked a policeman.

                                                      (CONTINUED)

57   CONTINUED:

                            POLICEMAN # 2
                          (a grim smile)
                       White men, Mr Quayle...

58   **EXT. GENERAL STORE, MARSABIT. DAY**   58

An image, as the policeman speaks, of what was seen: A GREEN
LONG WHEELBASE SAFARI TRUCK parked on a dusty road in glaring
sunshine. AN ATHLETIC, UNSHAVEN FAIR-HAIRED MAN returning to
the truck from the store, bottles of Oshodi in a box under
his arm. As he climbs into the truck we glimpse the driver: a
SQUAT, HARD-LOOKING BASTARD WITH A SHAVEN HEAD. They drive
off, squirting dust.

                        POLICEMAN # 2 (V.O.)
                     ...two of them, seen at Marsabit in
                     a green safari truck. They bought
                     Oshodi beer. They had a picnic
                     while they raped your wife. They
                     left the bottles.

59   **INT. POLICE STATION. DAY (CONTD.)**   59

                            JUSTIN
                     I know nothing of that.

                          POLICEMAN # 2
                     What did you ask this boy?

                            JUSTIN
                     His sister was being treated with
                     Dypraxa.

He waits for a reaction - fishing. There isn't one.

                         JUSTIN (CONT'D)
                     I expressed the hope it had done
                     her some good.

                          POLICEMAN # 1
                     For a diplomat you are not a very
                     good liar.

                            JUSTIN
                     I haven't risen very high.

As though on cue, the door flies open and SANDY strides in,
accompanied by D.I. DEASEY. The seated policeman rises.

                            SANDY
                       (coldly angry)
                     My name is Woodrow. Acting Head of
                     Mission for Her Majesty's
                     Government.
                          (MORE)

                                                          (CONTINUED)

59   CONTINUED: 59

                         SANDY (CONT'D)
              This is Detective-Inspector Deasey
              of Scotland Yard. Mr Deasey will be
              enquiring into the death of Mr
              Quayle's wife. If you have
              questions, ask them of him.
                   (to Justin)
              Have you been mistreated?

Justin shakes his head.

                         SANDY (CONT'D)
              Good. Then we'll go.

                         JUSTIN
                   (to Kenyan cop)
              Where is Kioko?
                   (to Sandy)
              The Kenyan boy I came to see.
                   (to cop)
              What have you done with him?

                         POLICEMAN # 1
              He ran away.

                         JUSTIN
              Let's hope nothing happens to him.
              I'll be back to check.

Leaving Deasey with the Kenyans, Sandy exits with Justin.

60   **EXT. POLICE STATION YARD. DAY**   60

Sandy and Justin emerge. Sandy's van is parked in the yard.
Justin's car has been moved next to it.

                         JUSTIN
              "Acting Head of Mission"?

                         SANDY
              Porter's been recalled - for
              "consultation".

                         JUSTIN
              Pity. I always liked Porter.

                         SANDY
              Everyone likes chaps who do
              nothing. They make no enemies.
                   (a beat)
              I'm flying the flag *pro tem*.
              Deasey's here to make sure Kenya's
              finest don't sweep anything under
              the carpet. Bluhm is one of theirs,
              after all.

                                              (CONTINUED)

                              JUSTIN
                    He's Belgian.

                              SANDY
                    Don't be obtuse, Justin. You know
                    what I mean.

                              JUSTIN
                    Is that the official thinking? That
                    Arnold did it?

                              SANDY
                    I'm afraid it's looking likely.

                              JUSTIN
                    Do you think he was her lover?

                              SANDY
                    I'm afraid that looks likely too.

                              JUSTIN
                    What were they doing at Lake
                    Turkana?

                              SANDY
                    Romantic setting. Sorry to have to
                    say it.

                              JUSTIN
                    Why suspect Bluhm, then? There
                    could have been others.
                         (off Sandy's questioning
                          look)
                    Other lovers. If she was an
                    unfaithful wife why stop at Arnold?

Sandy shifts uncomfortably. This is too close to home.

                              SANDY
                    You shouldn't listen to rumour.
                    Unless you've...evidence....

                              JUSTIN
                    Yes, evidence is always the
                    problem. You're discounting the two
                    Europeans seen at Marsabit?

                              SANDY
                    Circumstantial.

                              JUSTIN
                    Will Deasey want to interview me?

60   CONTINUED: (2)   60

                              SANDY
                    Shouldn't think so. Be a good man
                    and leave this to us, Justin. There
                    are proper channels for these
                    things.

61   **INT. UHURU HOSPITAL - ARCHIVE. DAY**   61

       Justin is with a HOSPITAL ADMINISTRATOR (about 50, dark
       suit), who is rummaging through the files.

                         HOSPITAL ADMINISTRATOR
                    Tessa Quayle I have...but I have no
                    Wanza Kilulu. Are you sure it is
                    the right name?

61A   **INT. UHURU HOSPITAL - CORRIDOR. DAY**   61A

       Justin and the hospital administrator are approaching the
       ward where Tessa lost her baby and Wanza died.

62   **INT. UHURU HOSPITAL - WARD. DAY**   62

       They enter the ward. Another PATIENT now occupies Wanza's bed
       but Tessa's remains empty, covered by a perished rubber
       sheet.

       JUSTIN stares at the empty bed, his emotions under tight
       control.

                              JUSTIN
                    There was a white doctor attending
                    her. Big chap, blond hair. Perhaps
                    he conducted the post mortem.

                         HOSPITAL ADMINISTRATOR
                    If there is no patient record how
                    can there be a post mortem record?
                         (a beat)
                    We have no European doctors here.

63   **INT. QUAYLES' HOUSE - BEDROOM. LATE DAY**   63

       Mustafa and Justin are working together in silence on either
       side of the bed. Stowing Tessa's clothes into plastic bags,
       presumably for distribution to charity.

       Justin draws the folds of a dress briefly to his face -
       Tessa's scent still on it - before carefully folding it away.

                              MUSTAFA
                    Why did Mama Tessa die?

       Justin looks up. Surprised by the question.

                                                        (CONTINUED)

                         JUSTIN
              We don't know, Mustafa.

                         MUSTAFA
              Dr Bluhm did not kill her.

                         JUSTIN
              No. He didn't.

                         MUSTAFA
              Was it because of this drug?

This stops Justin dead.

                         JUSTIN
              What drug?

                         MUSTAFA
              The drug they are testing in the
              villages.

                         JUSTIN
              What do you know about that?

                         MUSTAFA
              Mama Tessa and Dr Bluhm, they
              thought this drug was hurting
              people. I have heard them talking.
              They were writing a report about
              it.

This is news to Justin.

                         JUSTIN
              Do you know what they did with the
              report?

Mustafa shakes his head.

                         JUSTIN (CONT'D)
              Tell me what you heard.

                         MUSTAFA
                   (a shrug)
              They were afraid.

                         JUSTIN
              What of?

                         MUSTAFA
              People want to stop them.

                         JUSTIN
              Did they mention any names?

63   CONTINUED: (2)   63

Again Mustafa shakes his head. A pause, then:

                    MUSTAFA
          This drug, *bwana*. It is for TB?
                  (off Justin's nod)
          But it kills some people?

                    JUSTIN
          It seems so.

                    MUSTAFA
          But it helps some people?

                    JUSTIN
          Possibly. If it's a bad drug,
          Mustafa, it needs to be stopped.

                    MUSTAFA
                  (thoughtfully)
          If I had TB... if I was going to
          die of it...I would want this
          medicine.

ON JUSTIN

This is a perspective he hasn't been aware of before. It
gives him pause, as it should give us pause.

                                        CUT TO:

64   **EXT. RIVER ROAD. DAY**   64

DISCOVER GHITA walking along this crowded downtown Nairobi
street, an address in her hand. Looking for somewhere.

OVERLAP DIALOGUE

                    GHITA (V.O.)
          Why meet here, Justin? What mustn't
          we be seen talking about?

65   **INT. CAFE. DAY**   65

Justin and Ghita are at a table for two in a busy cafe
frequented exclusively by junior office workers. They're the
only non-Africans in the place.

                    JUSTIN
             Dypraxa.

Ghita tenses. Not a subject she wants to discuss anywhere.

                                              (CONTINUED)

>   JUSTIN (CONT'D)
>   Tessa and Arnold wrote a report -
>   on the ThreeBees trials. I need to
>   know what happened to it.

>   GHITA
>   What makes you think I know?

>   JUSTIN
>   They trusted you. So do I. Please
>   help me, Ghita.

>   GHITA
>   I know Tessa gave a copy to Sandy.

JUSTIN REACTS

>   JUSTIN
>   Why him?

>   GHITA
>   Sandy was a compromise. Semi-
>   official. Arnold wanted to go
>   public with it. Tessa wouldn't.

>   JUSTIN
>   Because?

>   GHITA
>   She wanted to do it your way.
>   Through channels. I wouldn't bother
>   looking for it, Justin. If it
>   threatens British commercial
>   interests it'll have been shredded.

>   JUSTIN
>   She could have brought it to me.

>   GHITA
>   She didn't want you involved.

>   JUSTIN
>   Why?
>   (off her silence)
>   Why didn't she want me involved?

>   GHITA
>   (quietly)
>   To protect you.

JUSTIN'S REACTION - of all the reasons Tessa might have had
for excluding him, this one hadn't occurred to Justin.

(CONTINUED)

CONTINUED: (2)

                         JUSTIN
          Who else did she show it to?

                         GHITA
          Kenny Curtiss. Handed it to him on
          his doorstep. She didn't tell me
          what he said but I can imagine. Ask
          Tim Donohue. They're pretty thick.
          They play golf together.

                                         CUT TO:

A NUMBER 9 IRON IN THE HANDS OF SIR KENNETH CURTISS

as it strikes the ball sweetly, lifting it out of a bunker
and dropping it onto one of the greens of

65A   ***EXT. NAIROBI GOLF COURSE. DAY***   65A

Crick trudging behind him with his golf bag, Curtiss joins
Donohue on the green. In the distance we might see other
WHITE PLAYERS, their CADDIES black to a man.

Curtiss's ball has landed about twelve feet from the hole;
Donohue's, we see, is closer.

Frowning with concentration, Curtiss lines up his putt...and
overshoots the hole by several feet.

                         DONOHUE
                    (crossing to his ball)
          Off your feed, Kenny?

                         CURTISS
          As if you didn't know.
                    (to Crick)
          Might help if you took the fucking
          flag out, Crick.

                         CRICK
          Get close enough to the fucking
          hole, maybe I will.

                         DONOHUE
          Interesting man you've got there,
          Kenny. I'd give odds Crick is the
          only white caddy in Africa.

                         CURTISS
          Never mind that. KDH are waiting
          for me to default on my Dypraxa
          commitments and I've got got a cash-
          flow problem. What are you lot
          going to do about it?

                                         (CONTINUED)

                    DONOHUE
           We never promised to protect you
           commercially.

He lines up his putt, but finds that Kenny has placed himself
directly behind the hole, along the line of the shot.

                    CURTISS
           <u>You</u> protect <u>me</u>! That's rich. A word
           in the right black ear from me,
           case of Krug, you'd be on the next
           plane home. I spend more on
           champagne in a year than your
           shop's annual fucking budget.

                    DONOHUE
           There you are, then. Cause of your
           cash-flow problem. You're in my eye-
           line, old man.

Curtiss doesn't move.

                    CURTISS
           Get your secret service to pull a
           few strings. What you buggers do,
           isn't it?

                    DONOHUE
           Is it? I'm never quite sure what it
           is we do.

Despite the distraction to his eye, Donohue takes his stroke.
The ball rolls towards the hole...

...until Curtiss steps forward and puts his foot on it.

                    CURTISS
           Don't even think about dumping me.
           I'm not a member of your fucking
           gentleman's club. I don't have to
           play by the rules.

                    DONOHUE
           So I see.
              (referring to his ball)
           Call that one "in", shall we?

He stoops to retrieve his ball. After a moment Curtiss
releases it. Donohue picks it up, and in doing so looks over
at Crick, who fails to meet his eye.

Curtiss strides off alone, Donohue wheezing several yards
behind with Crick.

                                            (CONTINUED)

65A   CONTINUED: (2)   65A

                         DONOHUE (CONT'D)
              Are they?

                         CRICK
              Are who what?

                         DONOHUE
              KDH. Hoping he'll default on his
              Dypraxa commitments.

                         CRICK
              I just carry his golf bag.

                         DONOHUE
                    (a smile)
              Of course you do.

65B   **EXT. GOLF COURSE - ANOTHER HOLE. DAY**   65B

We see Justin crossing the golf course towards the players.
Donohue makes an effort to reach Curtiss at the same time.

The direct face-to-face confrontation that follows, given
Justin's polite nature, is the equivalent of a punch in the
mouth.

                         JUSTIN
                    (to Curtiss)
              I believe you knew my wife.

                         DONOHUE
              Didn't know you were a member here,
              Justin.

But Justin and Curtiss are staring coldly at one another, too
absorbed even to hear him.

                         CURTISS
              Met her at one of your parties.

                         JUSTIN
              She came to see you. She gave you a
              report she'd written. On Dypraxa.

                         DONOHUE
              This isn't the time and place,
              Justin-

                         JUSTIN
                    (to Curtiss)
              I hope you didn't find her too
              troublesome. She could be a terrier
              when she had a scent.

                                              (CONTINUED)

65B   CONTINUED: 65B

                         CURTISS
               Sounds like you're describing a
               bitch.

          Justin works hard to keep his face from showing a reaction.
          Realizing he's gone too far, Curtiss pulls back a little.

                         CURTISS (CONT'D)
               I'm sorry about your loss. I don't
               remember being given any report.

                         JUSTIN
               Odd. She noted it in her diary.

                         CURTISS
               Then you know more than I do.

          Curtiss takes his shot, then strides off after the ball, with
          Crick following.

                         DONOHUE
               I didn't know Tessa kept a diary.

                         JUSTIN
               Seems Tessa was right, Tim.
               You don't know everything.

                         DONOHUE
                    (a smile)
               Oh I know where you're going
               Tuesday.

          A KENYAN crosses frame. Camera follows and

                                             REVERSES ANGLE
                                             TO REVEAL:

          The shanty town we recognise as KIBERA.

          AN AIRLINER CROSSES THE SKY

66A   **INT. AIRLINER COCKPIT. DAY**   66A

          We see CU cockpit instruments: map, time to destination etc.

66B   **JUSTIN'S POV ANGLE ON AIRPORT AS AIRLINER TOUCHES DOWN**   66B

67   **INT. LONDON AIRPORT PASSPORT CONTROL. EARLY MORNING**   67

          DISCOVER JUSTIN in the "EU PASSPORTS" line, among arriving
          EUROPEANS going through on the nod.

          In the "OTHER PASSPORTS" queue, BLACK KENYANS are being
          subjected to a far more rigorous scrutiny.

                                                          (CONTINUED)

67   CONTINUED: 67

Justin scarcely breaks stride as he flashes his passport at
the OFFICIAL on duty, expecting to be waved on. But the
official takes the passport from him and examines it.

                    IMMIGRATION OFFICIAL
          Welcome home, sir. Sorry about the
          weather.

                    JUSTIN
          Hardly your fault.

The official is holding Justin's passport up to the light.

                    IMMIGRATION OFFICIAL
          A while since you used this, is it?

                    JUSTIN
          About a year.

                    IMMIGRATION OFFICIAL
          Only we've had some forgeries on
          the diplomatics. I'm going to have
          to keep this, I'm afraid, sir.
          FCO'll issue you a new one.

67A   *JUSTIN POV FROM MOVING TAXI: OAK TREES IN A PARK*   67A

                    JUSTIN'S VOICE
          And if I want to travel?

                    IMMIGRATION OFFICIAL'S VOICE
          Only be a few days.

68   *EXT. GENTLEMEN'S CLUB, LONDON. DAY*   68

Justin has returned to a London winter, a foreign land of
chill drizzle and steamy car windows, like those on the taxi
now delivering him to a gentleman's club in St James's.

WORKMEN are digging a trench in front of the club, so the
cabbie is obliged to deposit Justin several feet from the
kerb. A CLUB DOORMAN in a top hat threads his way carefully
around the excavations to open the cab door for Justin.

PELLEGRIN, smiling a compassionate, welcoming smile, is
waiting by the porticoed entrance with a CLUB SERVANT.
Pellegrin clasps Justin's hand in both his own.

                    PELLEGRIN
          My dear fellow! What a dreadful
          time you've had. Welcome home.

                    JUSTIN
          Thank you, Bernard.

                                              (CONTINUED)

68   CONTINUED: 68

The servant stretches out his hand to take Justin's bag.

                    CLUB SERVANT
          Allow me, sir.

                    JUSTIN
          Thank you, I'd rather keep it with
          me.

The servant's eyes flick to Pellegrin for guidance.

                    PELLEGRIN
          Club rule, Justin. No luggage in
          the dining room.

Arm around Justin's shoulders, Pellegrin propels him inside.

The servant moves off with the bag towards a side entrance.

69   **INT. CLUB CORRIDOR. DAY**   69

As Pellegrin walks Justin towards the dining room:

                    PELLEGRIN
          Any plans yet or is it too soon?

                    JUSTIN
          Plans?

                    PELLEGRIN
          Holidays, visiting friends, million
          things you've always wanted to do
          in the garden. You're on indefinite
          sick leave. Enjoy it. I hear the
          snow's good at Chamonix.

                    JUSTIN
          I don't have a passport, Bernard.
          They took mine at the airport.

                    PELLEGRIN
          Of course. You missed the recall.

70   **INT. CLUB DINING ROOM. DAY**   70

"Home" for Pellegrin is a granite-pillared dining room; grey-
suited WHITEHALL MANDARINS dining under a painted heaven of
cherubs posturing in a sky-blue ceiling. His preferred corner
table is sheltered by a dracaena palm.

A WEST INDIAN WAITER in a mauve dinner jacket provides menus,
then glides silently away.

                                              (CONTINUED)

>   PELLEGRIN
> The sole meunière's not bad here,
> if you like sole. Otherwise have it
> grilled.

>   JUSTIN
> Meunière would be fine.

>   PELLEGRIN
> No starters, I think.

Pellegrin ticks two boxes on an order pad with his name
printed at the top. He slides it under the salt cellar.

>   PELLEGRIN (CONT'D)
> You're cleared, by the way. Thought
> we'd get that bit of unpleasantness
> dealt with first.

>   JUSTIN
> Cleared for what?

>   PELLEGRIN
> Of what. Murder most foul. Seems
> you didn't hire contract killers in
> some den of vice after all.
> Deasey's satisfied it was a crime
> of passion by our dark medical
> horse. Just a question now of
> finding Bluhm.

The waiter glides partially INTO SHOT, takes the order and
glides OUT OF SHOT.

>   JUSTIN
> Arnold Bluhm is gay, Bernard. Gay
> men don't rape their women friends.

>   PELLEGRIN
> I've known one or two very savage
> queens in my time. Do you no good
> to go poking around under rocks,
> Justin. Some nasty things live
> under rocks, especially in foreign
> gardens. Advice of a friend.

>   JUSTIN
> What is it I'm not to look into?

>   PELLEGRIN
> Quayles have always made reliable
> Foreign Service men.
>   (MORE)

                    PELLEGRIN (CONT'D)
          Shouldn't be surprised if there
          were a small Head of Mission still
          in your knapsack. Not many of our
          sort left, more's the pity.

                    JUSTIN
          Isn't Porter Coleridge one of our
          sort?

                    PELLEGRIN
          You're wondering why we brought him
          home. Heading a new development aid
          department. Challenging post.

                    JUSTIN
          More challenging than dealing with
          Kenny Curtiss?

                    PELLEGRIN
          Crude sort of chap, our Kenny, but
          he flies the flag for us. Got up
          dear Tessa's nose, I fear.

                    JUSTIN
          Yes, she wrote a report about it.

                    PELLEGRIN
          About Kenny?

                    JUSTIN
          Dypraxa.

                    PELLEGRIN
          Ah. That.

                    JUSTIN
          She expected some action to be
          taken. None was, was it?

                    PELLEGRIN
          She tell you about the letter? Or
          did you find it among her things?
          Tucked into her diary, perhaps.

                    JUSTIN
          Which letter was that, Bernard?

                    PELLEGRIN
          Ramblings of an ageing fart.
          Senility setting in early, alas.
          Naughty of her to take it. Very
          naughty indeed.

                    JUSTIN
          Yes, I found that.

                         PELLEGRIN
              Be grateful to have it back.
              Written under stress, you
              understand. Regrettable things
              said. Wouldn't want it falling into
              the wrong hands.

A flash of puzzlement crosses Justin's face. The only
compromising letter he knows of is Sandy's declaration of
love for Tessa, and his own hands are the worst possible for
that to have fallen into.

                         JUSTIN
              Sorry, Bernard, are we talking
              about the same letter?

                         PELLEGRIN
              What's yours about?

                         JUSTIN
              Undying love.

                         PELLEGRIN
              Ah.

The waiter lays a sole meunière before Pellegrin and a
grilled sole in front of Justin.

                         JUSTIN
              Why, what's yours?

                         PELLEGRIN
              They're not so good grilled. You
              should have had the meunière.

CU GRILLED SOLE

CU FISH AND CHIPS IN GREASY NEWSPAPER

                        PULL BACK TO:

71   ***INT. TUBE STATION. DAY***   71

The fish and chips are a SECURITY GUARD'S lunch, being eaten
in a small office. There is a bank of security monitors on
which can be seen, amongst others, JUSTIN being met and
hugged by ARTHUR LUIGI HAMMOND (HAM).

OUTSIDE ON THE CONCOURSE

JUSTIN is being violently hugged by HAM, a pink-faced cuddly
man with twinkly eyes, bundled up in a voluminous brown
overcoat. He is, Tessa's first cousin (mid-30's).

Tears are coursing down Ham's face. The crowd divides to flow around them like a river around a boulder.

                    JUSTIN
               (with feeling)
          Good to see you again, Ham.

                    HAM
          Sorry about the blubbing. It's
          those damned Latin genes.

                    JUSTIN
          Same old Ham.

                    HAM
          Oh no. Not any more.

71A   **EXT. LONDON STREET. DAY**   71A

They start to walk towards Ham's offices, Justin constantly scanning the lunchtime crowds for signs of surveillance.

VARIOUS ANGLES ON UNOBTRUSIVE PASSERS-BY, POSSIBLE WATCHERS – could be anyone – in a car, on a bike, on foot....

                    JUSTIN
          How have you been?

                    HAM
          Miserable. Desperate. You know how
          close I was to Tess.

                    JUSTIN
          Yes, I do know.

                    HAM
          First cousins can be closer than
          siblings. Still don't understand
          why I let you talk me out of going
          to the funeral. Doesn't sit right.

                    JUSTIN
          Wrong crowd for you, Ham. We'll
          have a private memorial service
          here. You can blub all the way
          through it.

                    HAM
          Don't think I won't. Hire the
          Abbey. You can afford it now.

                    JUSTIN
               (distracted, watching)
          Can I?

                                          (CONTINUED)

                  HAM
        Tess left you bloody well off. Want
        to know what you're worth?

                  JUSTIN
        Not particularly.

                  HAM
        I haven't sold the Chelsea house.
        Thought you might want to stay
        there while you're in London-

                  JUSTIN
        No.

                  HAM
        Well, it's yours anyway - that and
        her African women's charity. Said
        it'd get you out of the garden.

                  JUSTIN
        When did she say that?

                  HAM
        Two weeks before she died.
          (pause)
        Have you had lunch?

                  JUSTIN
        Yes, a very civilized lunch with
        Bernard Pellegrin. At which he
        expressed interest in Tessa's
        diary.

                  HAM
        Tess never kept a diary. Hated the
        things.

                  JUSTIN
        You and I know that. Pellegrin must
        have been disinformed.

72   **INT. HAMMOND MANZINI OFFICES. DAY**   72

A retro enclave in a modern building. The walls are hung with
fading images of the illustrious dead and a single enlarged
photograph in a silver frame, showing a 16 YEAR-OLD HAM and a
7 YEAR-OLD TESSA with their AUNT CORINA (50) in Pisa.

Ham is seated at an ancient desk, taking delivery of a take-
away lunch from a CHINESE DELIVERY BOY. He immediately starts
to open the tinfoil cartons.

Justin is looking out of the window.

(CONTINUED)

Through the open door of an adjacent room ELECTRONIC BEEPS
and CRASHES can be heard. Someone playing a computer game.

>   HAM
>   Tess thought she was being watched.
>   How do you tell?

>   JUSTIN
>   In a civilized country you can't.
>   It's done subtly - a confiscated
>   passport, a club servant going
>   through your bag while you lunch.

>   HAM
>   Not my game, thank God. Sooner play
>   billiards.
>   (indicating next-door)
>   Or whatever that is Guido's doing.
>   (calling)
>   Come and have some lunch.
>   (to Justin)
>   I warned Tess about it. Didn't stop
>   her e-mailing twice a day. More
>   enquiries than Google. Got behind
>   in my work answering them all. Act
>   of love, you see. I loved her
>   rotten.

>   JUSTIN
>   And she loved you rotten. Enquiries
>   about what?

A plump, pink 12 year-old boy now enters the room - GUIDO,
Ham's son. He makes straight for the Chinese dishes and
unceremoniously helps himself, competing with his father for
the noodles.

>   HAM
>   Look at him. Boy's two-thirds
>   machine. Mind of a computer,
>   appetite of a waste disposal.
>   (to Guido)
>   Aren't you?

Guido grins, stuffing his face regardless.

>   JUSTIN
>   What's the other third?

>   HAM
>   Manzini. Unquestionably.
>   (to Guido)
>   Those e-mails from Tess...
>   (MORE)

72   CONTINUED: (2)

                         HAM (CONT'D)
                    (to Justin)
               Guido helped me with them.

                         GUIDO
               Company stuff. Bo-ring.

                         HAM
               Ownership, franchises, that sort of
               thing. Trying to find out who
               brokered the marriage.

                         JUSTIN
               What marriage?

                         HAM
               KDH and ThreeBees. KDH make
               Dypraxa, ThreeBees test it. It's a
               marriage of convenience, of course.
               Both in it for what they can get
               out of it.

JUSTIN REACTS - jolted by the phrase.

                         JUSTIN
               Her phrase or yours?

                         HAM
               Oh, hers.

ON JUSTIN - visibly relieved. Not a reference to him and
Tessa after all.

                         JUSTIN
               "Producing dead offspring."

73   *INT. SIDE OFFICE. DAY*   73

Justin and Ham are now standing one on either side of Guido,
who is back at the computer keyboard accessing the emails
Tessa sent them.

                         JUSTIN
               Pity we can't get at what was on
               her computer.

                         GUIDO
               Why not?

                         JUSTIN
                    (slightly patronising)
               It was stolen, Guido.

                         GUIDO
                    (with a gesture)
               So?

                                                    (CONTINUED)

Justin is amazed. Didn't imagine it was possible.

>   GUIDO (CONT'D)
>   I can get that stuff through her
>   server. All you need's the
>   password.

>   JUSTIN
>   I don't know the password.

>   GUIDO
>   (flaps his lips with his
>   fingers.)
>   Duh. Five letters, Juss. Three
>   guesses.

Justin shakes his head.

>   GUIDO (CONT'D)
>   My name, yeah? Use a One for the
>   "I", zero for the "O".

He leans over and types in: "G-U-1-D-0" (sic)...

...and Tessa's desktop pops onto the screen.

Now his fingers fly over the keyboard like a concert
pianist's and we jolt suddenly into Tessa's world, via the
public markers to her private passions: BUKO, Pharma Watch,
WHO, Hippo etc.: a rush to the head - a verbal, aural,
pictorial flow of superhighway information that flashes past
faster than Justin's mind can absorb.

>   HAM
>   Give him a chance to read it.

>   GUIDO
>   Lightning tour. I'm printing out as
>   I go.

ANGLE ON THE HIGH-SPEED OFFICE PRINTER already starting to
disgorge hard copies of the various e-mails and websites, the
documents rapidly piling up in the tray.

>   JUSTIN
>   What's Hippo?

>   HAM
>   Oh, I know that one. German Pharma
>   Watch - keeps an eye on what the
>   drug companies are up to.

>   JUSTIN
>   Can we open that?

(CONTINUED)

Guido does so. A list of documents appears and a computer
version of the photograph we saw in Tessa's lacquered box:
Birgit and her toddler son Karl. This, too, we see emerging
from the printer with the other material.

                                      WE PAN BACK TO:

THE COMPUTER SCREEN where among the more serious stuff, Guido
is now bringing up a number of personal Webcam messages:
Tessa singing "Happy Birthday" to Guido in Italian; Tessa
"gurning" to Guido and Ham; Guido and Ham pulling grotesque
faces back. But we also see some of Tessa's questions to Ham:
"Ham, I need more on the Dypraxa patents..."; "Sorry,
darling, just an itty-bitty bit more about KDH corporate
structure..."; "Ham, my sweet, please-pretty-please? Company
structure of ThreeBees..?"

A NET MESSENGER CONVERSATION between TESSA and BIRGIT, seen
via SPLIT-SCREEN WEBCAM IMAGES

                    TESSA (WEBCAM)
          Hi, Birgit. Sorry, more questions.
          Tessa never sleeps.

                    BIRGIT (WEBCAM)
          Always time for you, Tessa...

The images disappear as Guido returns to Tessa's Desktop and
pulls down her favourites list and here we see the KDH icon.
Justin's finger comes INTO SHOT and settles on it.

                    JUSTIN
          KDH, I want that one.

                    GUIDO
          Sure. No probs.

He clicks...

...and THE KDH HOME PAGE appears: a revolving banner graphic
of molecular structures, happy patients, Third World
treatment centres; a site map with buttons for: "ABOUT KDH",
"CONTACT US", "PRODUCTS IN DEVELOPMENT", "KDH CANADA", "KDH
SWITZERLAND", "ACHIEVEMENTS", "KDH WORLDWIDE".

Inset is a picture, headlined: "KDH BRINGS 1,500 JOBS TO
WALES". Topping the new plant: the trademark KDH steeple (a
towering stainless steel sculpture representing a hypodermic
needle). Below: several tiny human figures at a ribbon-
cutting ceremony.

                    JUSTIN
                 (pointing)
          Is it possible to magnify that?

                                            (CONTINUED)

  73

                         HAM
              Magnify it? He can send it out for
              doughnuts.
                    (pats Guido's head
                    proudly)
              My boy here's got the full fifteen-
              second attention span. None of his
              friends get beyond ten.

Justin leans over to peer more closely at the image as Guido
enlarges it with a series of zooms. Thus we identify PHIL
McKENZIE at the UK HEALTH MINISTER's elbow as the latter cuts
the ribbon. McKenzie's name and title appear below the
picture: "PHIL McKENZIE, CHAIRMAN OF KDH".

Behind McKenzie is another figure, too small to be
identified.

Again Justin points.

                         JUSTIN
              Can you zoom in on that?

Guido zooms in to maximum enlargement. A fuzzy but
recognisable face appears:

PELLEGRIN

                         JUSTIN (CONT'D)
              My God! She knew how to choose her
              enemies.

ANGLE ON GUIDO

As Guido finds and cannot resist clicking on a file labelled
"TOP SECRET KEEP OUT"

                         HAM (V.O.)
              You know Tess, never thought small.

ON THE SCREEN has appeared the image of Tessa in her bubble
bath filmed by Justin, which Tessa has cut together with
footage of Justin sleeping and her affectionate comments
over.

Seeing this footage for the first time and Justin's emotional
reaction to it, Ham steers Guido out of the room leaving
Justin alone.

73A   **INT. HAM'S OFFICE. DAY**   73A

Justin is sorting and reading emails at Ham's desk. One in
particular has taken his attention.

                                                  (CONTINUED)

73A   CONTINUED: 73A

> HAM (V.O.)
> Wondered when you'd find that one.

INSERT EMAIL:

"Moral dilemma, Ham, and the person I most want to tell can't be told. Had a..."

> TESSA'S VOICE (V.O.)
> ...Had a creepy love letter today,
> from a poor guy I've cold-bloodedly
> led on...

TESSA'S VOICE CARRIES OVER TO:

74   ***EXT. TESSA'S CHELSEA HOUSE. DUSK***   74

The front garden run wild, the house closed up.

JUSTIN peering in through a ground-floor window.

HIS POV: AN ABANDONED ROOM, its furniture shrouded in dust sheets. Couldn't stay there, couldn't stay away.

> TESSA'S VOICE
> ...I stole something from him and -
> worse - made him a vile promise
> I've no intention of keeping...

As Justin moves away from the house towards its overgrown back garden, security lights come on, tripped by his presence.

ANGLE ON BACK GARDEN - harshly lit by the security lights. Flowers dead on the stalk, long weed-choked grass. To the gardener in Justin it's a distressing sight.

We see a single mature oak, the remains of Tessa's childhood tree house: part of her life Justin never shared.

Settling himself beneath the oak, Justin pulls from his pocket the e-mail printout we saw in Ham's office.

> TESSA'S VOICE
> ...I hate to think how it would
> hurt Justin if he knew. I've
> violated his code, Ham, in the most
> cynical way...

Instinctively Justin reaches out to dead-head a rose. Probably unaware he's doing it. He crumples its brittle petals in his fist.

74   CONTINUED: 74

                    TESSA'S VOICE
              And the end that justifies my
              means? I need this guy to help me
              blackmail HMG. Tell me I'm not a
              ruthless bitch. Tell me Justin
              would understand. Wrong answer and
              I'll push you into the Tiber as I
              did when you were sixteen. *Ciao*,
              darling.

ANGLE ON THE NEGLECTED GARDEN

                                      MATCH DISSOLVE
                                      TO:

THE SAME GARDEN, WELL TENDED AND IN FULL DAYLIGHT

75   **INT. TESSA'S BEDROOM/CONSERVATORY. DAY(TWO YEARS EARLIER)**   75

The room reflects Tessa's contrasting nature: casually
inherited wealth at ease with a far-from-casually acquired
radicalism. Posters espousing Third World/feminist causes
hang on the walls side by side with listed paintings, among
them the *Madonna and Child* and the water colour of the
Manzini mansion, both seen in the Quayles' Nairobi house.
Polemical works and the latest annual report of *Amnesty
International* share space on her bookshelves with children's
classics and legal volumes. But there's also a Hepplewhite
chair and writing desk; a silk Persian rug: tasteful,
valuable items indicative of refined taste.

DISCOVER TESSA AND JUSTIN

side by side in her double bed, in satisfied post-coital
silence.

                    JUSTIN
              Thank you.

Tessa looks at him with mock-puzzled amusement.

                    TESSA
              For?

Her response unbalances him.

                    JUSTIN
              This. It's been a wonderful...
              gift.

                    TESSA
              How generous of me.

                                              (CONTINUED)

STILLS

Rachel Weisz as Tessa Quayle and Ralph Fiennes as her husband, Justin Quayle.
(photographs by Jaap Buitendijk)

Justin Quayle (Ralph Fiennes) says farewell at the airfield to Tessa (Rachel Weisz) and Arnold Bluhm (Hubert Koundé) as they head off to Loki.

Tessa Quayle (Rachel Weisz) desperately wants to improve the health conditions in Kenya.

Sandy Woodrow (Danny Huston), head of Chancery, British High Commission, in Nairobi, Kenya.

Justin (Ralph Fiennes) tries to decipher Tessa's computer files.

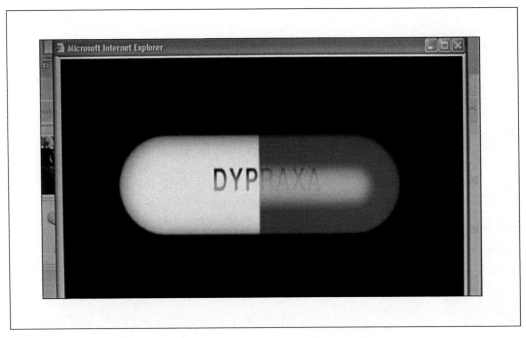

The drug Dypraxa may hold the biggest clue in this mystery.

Justin (Ralph Fiennes) follows the murderous trail to Berlin.

Justin is attacked in his hotel and threatened one more time.

Justin (Ralph Fiennes) confronts Sandy Woodrow in the garden in Nairobi.

Justin (Ralph Fiennes), Lorbeer (Pete Postlethwaite), and Nemo flee from the marauding tribesmen.

The plane just makes it out of the village, taking Justin to Lake Turkana.

Cinematographer César Charlone with director Fernando Meirelles.

Ralph Fiennes and Rachel Weisz with director Fernando Meirelles.

                         JUSTIN
              No, of course, I don't mean... That
              is... One hopes it was reciprocal.
              Not that I'd assumed...

                         TESSA
              That you gave me pleasure?

                         JUSTIN
              You know what I mean.

She laughs. Can't keep it up.

                         TESSA
              In that case, thank you too.
                   (pause)
              So who is this Justin Quayle I've
              taken to my bed and why isn't there
              a Mrs Quayle and two-point-five
              little assorted Quayles at prep
              school?

                         JUSTIN
              I've sent back one or two potential
              Mrs Quayles. No children reported.

                         TESSA
                   (taps his lip reprovingly)
              Diplomat's answer. Non-committal.

                         JUSTIN
              I'm not sure a decision to be
              uncommitted is quite the same as
              being non-committal.

                         TESSA
              Sir Bernard answer.

                         JUSTIN
                   (fondling her)
              Tessa Prior response.

                         TESSA
              Ah, well. Tessa Prior's blunt and
              rude, we all know that. Can't think
              what she's doing in bed with a
              diplomat.

                         JUSTIN
              It isn't the diplomat who's in bed
              with you.

                         TESSA
              Oh, who is?

> JUSTIN
> A reckless older man.

> TESSA
> Not so reckless.
> (a beat)
> I feel safe with you.

> JUSTIN
> Flirting with an older man who
> admires her spirit.

> TESSA
> I flirt with men I feel safe with.
> (beat)
> Or if it gets me what I want.
> (beat)
> Sometimes they're the same.

Kissing her lightly, Justin swings his legs over the side, only to realise that he must now stand and cross the room naked to where, discarded in the press of passion, his clothes are lying.

Tessa comes to his aid by handing him, teasingly, from her side of the bed, a gaily-patterned pink silk kimono.

Justin puts it on and stands – to her amusement – with no evident loss of dignity, clad only in this unequivocally feminine garment. Glancing towards the conservatory, he picks up a bottle of Evian water from the bedside table.

> JUSTIN
> I suppose when you were six you led
> the class revolt.

> TESSA
> No, I was a very conventional
> little girl. I climbed trees and
> bashed cheeky boys – English and
> Italian.
> (off his reaction)
> When I wasn't here I was on Elba,
> pretending to be Napoleon.
> (gestures at the
>   watercolour)
> My mother was the twelfth Contessa
> Manzini.

> JUSTIN
> (touches forelock)
> My lady.

(CONTINUED)

75   CONTINUED: (3)   75

                              TESSA
                   Am I?

                              JUSTIN
                   Can you see another?

He carries the water bottle into the conservatory and sets to
watering the pot plants. He fingers the yellowed leaves of an
African Violet, clucking with disapproval.

                              JUSTIN (CONT'D)
                   If these were children they'd be
                   taken into care. And you'd be
                   prosecuted.

                              TESSA
                      (amused)
                   I do water them. When I remember.

                              JUSTIN
                   "I do feed my babies, Your Worship.
                   When I remember."

Tenderly he detaches a dead leaf. Tessa smiles fondly.

BACK TO PRESENT-DAY SCENE

                              JUSTIN (CONT'D)
                   Forgive me...

He rests his head between his hands.

He has come, at last, to that private place he has been
seeking. And here the e-mail's final vindication of Tessa
bursts the dam. The weight of Justin's grief, so long held
back by suspicion and doubt, now floods through the breach
with astonishing violence, racking every muscle of his body.
He sobs as though vomiting up his pain: a poison of which the
body must purge itself before action....

VARIOUS SHOTS of Justin making a futile attempt to repair two
years' neglect to Tessa's garden, his mind, as he does so, is
absorbing, planning, building resolve to do what he is now
free to do.

75A   *INT. TESSA'S BEDROOM. DUSK.*   75A

The room, like the garden, has seen two years' neglect. Gone
are the plants, the pictures from the walls, the small marks
and reminders of Tessa's personality.

Justin sits on Tessa's bare bed, pulls a mobile 'phone from
his pocket and dials a number.

                                                      (CONTINUED)

                        JUSTIN
             Ham... Do you still represent that
             dodgy client in Amsterdam?

76   **INT. LONDON RAIL TERMINUS. MORNING**   76

The train is about to depart. Doors are slammed, a GUARD
checks his watch, whistle poised in his mouth.

DISCOVER JUSTIN on the platform, bag in hand. But he can't
board yet; he's waiting for something, someone....

...HAM tearing through the barrier, the tails of his overcoat
flapping; puffing mightily as he propels his bulk half the
platform's length to a Justin much relieved to see him.

Red-faced and with hardly breath enough left for speech, Ham
thrusts a small manila envelope into Justin's hand.

                      HAM
               (breathless)
           Sorry...only just got it....
               (breath)
           Directions for use - no air travel,
           no credit cards...never say your
           name on the phone or the
           computers'll kick in....
               (breath)
           Dodgy Client adds: "Welcome to my
           world."

                      JUSTIN
           I don't want his world.

                      HAM
           No choice, old chum. Actually, I'm
           getting a bit paranoid myself. I've
           put an address inside. Aunt Corina,
           the old bat in Rome. If you need to
           contact me you'd better do it
           through her. She adored Tess.

                      JUSTIN
           I failed her, Ham. I lost my faith
           in her. Now it's too late.

                      HAM
           She forgives you. She loved you
           rotten too, you know.
               (a beat)
           Look, suppose I posited that all
           this is co-incidental.
               (MORE)

                                             (CONTINUED)

76   CONTINUED: 76

                          HAM (CONT'D)
              Tess killed by bandits, pure and
              simple, and that you're being as
              paranoid as she was. Any credence
              in that for you?

Justin reaches into his pocket, extracts a folded sheet of
paper. He unfolds it for Ham to see.

INSERT DEATH THREAT: Typewritten in thick black capitals:
"STOP NOW OR GET WHAT YOUR WIFE GOT"

Ham shrugs. Tried.

                          JUSTIN
              Thanks for trying, Ham. But I have
              to finish what she started.

With another great bear-hug he and Justin part, Ham once
again unashamedly free with his tears.

76A   ***EXT. WIDE ANGLE ESTABLISHING SHOT OF NAIROBI. DAY***   76A

77   ***INT. HIGH COMMISSION, NAIROBI. DAY***   77

Sandy Woodrow is addressing a plenary staff meeting.

                          SANDY
              It seems our erstwhile colleague
              has disappeared....

FAVOURING GHITA AND DONOHUE, seated next to one another.

                          SANDY (CONT'D)
              Four days ago he lunched in London
              with the Pellegrin, who describes
              him as overwrought, after which he
              visited his wife's lawyer before
              going off our radar...

Murmurings from the audience. During this somebody's mobile
'phone rings and is hurriedly silenced.

                          SANDY (CONT'D)
              The poor man has convinced himself
              there was a conspiracy against
              Tessa, in which we were all
              complicit....

                          DONOHUE
              Those whom the Gods would destroy
              they first make mad.

Said softly to himself, but wanting Ghita to hear.

                                                    (CONTINUED)

                              SANDY
              If he __has__ left the U.K. he did so
              without a passport. Therefore, any
              contact from Justin __must__ be
              reported to me immediately, in his
              own best interest.

In the general babble of conversation that follows:

                              DONOHUE
              No point asking if you've heard
              from him, I suppose?

                              GHITA
              No, Tim, none at all.

Donohue smiles appreciatively. Axiom of his trade: better an
honest adversary than a mendacious ally.

                                            CUT TO:

77A   __EXT. BERLIN - SIEGESSAULE/VICTORY MONUMENT. DAY__   77A

77B   __EXT. BERLIN RAILWAY STATION/STREETS. DAY__   77B

Justin exits the station.

Now walking past a mural.

                        TESSA'S VOICE (V.O.)
              Birgit, why are ThreeBees spending
              70 million dollars developing
              Dypraxa for KDH?

78   __EXT. HIPPO HQ. MORNING__   78

He crosses past A GERMAN POLICE CAR parked outside a turreted
five-storey corner house.

                        TESSA'S VOICE
              Is the African market worth that
              much?

The exterior of the house is decorated with bright murals of
Third World children. A green hippo is painted on the front
door, which stands ajar; above it the words "PHARMA WATCH
INTERNATIONAL".

DISCOVER JUSTIN entering the building.

                        BIRGIT (V.O.)
              Tessa, you have to understand the
              scale of this. There is a TB
              epidemic coming.
                        (MORE)

                                              (CONTINUED)

78   CONTINUED:

                         BIRGIT (V.O.) (CONT'D)
                It will affect the entire world.
                Big Pharma smells big money.
                America is their market, not
                Africa...

79   **_INT. HIPPO OFFICE. MORNING_**   79

On the way in Justin has stopped to look at various posters
displayed on the walls, most of them in English. We might
see, for example:

A CARTOON depicting a white-coated figure wearing a
stethoscope and devil's horns, his top pocket bulging with
dollars as he injects a child. Caption: "DOCTORS ARE NOT
SAINTS! MEDICAL OPINION CAN BE BOUGHT!"

Another cartoon - set in a circus ring - has a figure in
spangled tights labelled "U.S. PHARMACEUTICAL" balancing on
the shoulders of Uncle Sam, who is balancing in turn on a
tiny, crushed dark-skinned figure labelled "GENERIC DRUGS".
Captioned: "THE WORLD'S GREATEST PHILANTHROPIST ACT".

                         TESSA (V.O.)
                If the market's elsewhere, why test
                in Africa?

                         BIRGIT (V.O.)
                New drugs have to be tried
                somewhere, Tessa. They go where
                they can buy patients for pennies,
                nobody sues, nobody complains about
                missing bodies...

Entering the main office, Justin finds a familiar chaos:
shelves and filing cabinets emptied, contents dumped on the
floor; desks bearing tell-tale clean rectangles where once
stood computers.

A UNIFORMED POLICEMAN is taking a statement from a distraught
young SECRETARY. Nobody else is in the office.

                         SECRETARY
                    (to Justin, in German)
                I'm sorry, we're closed.
                [Es tut mir leid, aber wir haben
                geschlossen.]

                         JUSTIN
                I'm looking for Birgit.
                [Ich suche Birgit.]

                         SECRETARY
                We have had a burglary. Nobody is
                here. Come back tomorrow.
                [Wir hatten einen Einbruch.
                         (MORE)

                                                        (CONTINUED)

79   CONTINUED:

                         SECRETARY (CONT'D)
                 Es ist niemand hier. Kommen Sie
                 morgen wieder.]

                         JUSTIN
                 I really would like to see her
                 today if at all possible.
                 [Ich muss sie aber unbedingt heute
                 sehen.]

                         SECRETARY
                     (suspicious)
                 I cannot give out a home address.
                 [Ich darf keine Privatadresse
                 rausgeben.]

                         POLICEMAN
                 You are?
                 [Wie ist Ihr Name?]

                         JUSTIN
                 Michael Adams.
                     (to secretary, hoping
                      she'll catch on)
                 Tessa's husband.
                 [Tessas Ehemann.]

The policeman holds out his hand. Into it Justin places his
passport. To the secretary he offers the Birgit-Karl
photograph.

The policeman briefly checks the passport then hands it back,
satisfied that the name matches the face - his only concern.

The secretary, by contrast, returns the Birgit-Karl photo
with a smile. The suspicion has left her face.

                         SECRETARY
                 She collects Karl at three. From
                 the kindergarten in *Bahnhofstrasse*.
                 [Sie holt Karl um drei ab. Vom
                 Kindergarten in der Bahnhofstraße.]

80   **EXT. KINDERGARTEN. DAY**   80

The kindergarten is situated on one side of a wide street;
cars containing waiting MOTHERS parked on both sides. In
front of the building, which has its own outdoor play area,
is a pedestrian crossing, patrolled by a CROSSING GUARD.
Opposite there is a grassy area on which THREE YOUTHS are
kicking a football about, shouting raucously.

SOUND OVER: SIXTY LITTLE VOICES SINGING A CHILD'S ECOLOGICAL
PROTEST SONG (about destruction of unrecoverable resources?).

81   *INT. KINDERGARTEN ANTE-ROOM. DAY*   81

The singing comes to us through a glass wall from an adjacent
playroom, but the room we're seeing should reflect the
"alternative" character of the kindergarten (this being where
Hippo's staff send their kids). Thus: a frieze of "Children
of the World", a collage of endangered natural resources -
cut-outs of trees, whales, etc - but arranged in rows like
markers in a graveyard.

> TESSA (V.O.)
> Okay, then why ThreeBees? Why a
> British firm?

> BIRGIT (V.O.)
> We wonder this too. Tessa, if the
> trials bankrupt the bees the
> African rights will revert to KDH.
> They win either way.

> TESSA (V.O.)
> Thanks, *liebchen*. Kiss Karl for me.
> *Ciao*.

> BIRGIT (V.O.)
> *Ciao*, Tessa.

WITH A SUDDEN RUSH OF SOUND AND MOVEMENT the doors to the
adjoining room burst open and SIXTY UNDER-FIVES pour in.

Simultaneously as many MOTHERS, FATHERS, AUNTS, NANNIES,
GRANNIES and BIG SISTERS - among them JUSTIN - surge into the
ante-room from the street.

ANGLE ON BIRGIT as she finds KARL among the outpouring kids.

ANGLE ON JUSTIN approaching her through the throng. He shows
the photograph.

> JUSTIN
> You sent this to my wife.

BIRGIT'S REACTION is cautious, more fearful than welcoming.

> BIRGIT
> Justin?

> JUSTIN
> I need to talk to you.

Birgit shakes her head.

(CONTINUED)

CONTINUED:

> BIRGIT
> Our computers were stolen last
> night. They have never gone this
> far before. I can't be seen with
> you. I have Karl to think of.

> JUSTIN
> Where would be a safe place?

> BIRGIT
> Nowhere. Nowhere is safe.

She glances around her at the dozens of mothers and under-
fives heading in an untidy stream for the door.

> BIRGIT (CONT'D)
> (sudden realisation)
> Here. Now, with these people.

Taking Karl by the hand, she joins the throng moving towards
the street. Justin goes with her, not quite understanding.

> BIRGIT (CONT'D)
> In this crowd we can talk. My
> bicycle is across the street. Ask
> your questions before we get to it.

82   **EXT. KINDERGARTEN/STREET. DAY**   82

THE EMERGING CROWD - FAVOURING BIRGIT, JUSTIN, KARL as they
move through the outdoor play area to the crossing, where the
crossing guard is bunching the group, holding them until
there are enough to take across.

> JUSTIN
> Is it a scam?

> BIRGIT
> Scam?

> JUSTIN
> Dypraxa. Does it cure TB?

> BIRGIT
> Yes, it cures. Instead of eight
> months of intensive treatment you
> swallow twelve little tablets...

A ball rolls in front of them, kicked by one of TWO TOUGH-
LOOKING YOUTHS playing football in the play area. Birgit and
Justin hesitate long enough to allow the ball to be retrieved
before moving on. They pass under an arch.

82   CONTINUED: 82

                              JUSTIN
                    So what's the problem?

                              BIRGIT
                    It cures. But it also kills.
                         (off his look)
                    They haven't the formula right yet.
                    To go back to the lab would cost
                    them two years and millions of
                    dollars. Other companies would have
                    time to produce their own cure.
                    Next question?

                              JUSTIN
                    You said in your e-mails the Kenyan
                    government approved the trials...

                              BIRGIT
                    Somebody bribed them.

                              JUSTIN
                    Who?

                              BIRGIT
                         (a shrug)
                    ThreeBees? Lorbeer? Who knows? Put
                    $50,000 in the right hands and you
                    can test battery acid as skin
                    lotion.

They have reached the road. The crossing guard has been
holding up traffic. Now she waves the group across. Holding
Karl's hand, Birgit steps into the roadway. Justin takes the
little boy's free hand. Karl looks up at him and smiles.

                              JUSTIN
                    The deaths - how do they hide the
                    bodies?

                              BIRGIT
                    In Africa? Who cares? Next?

                              JUSTIN
                    Who is Lorbeer?

She looks up. A motor cycle with a pillion passenger is
roaring towards the crossing...

Instinctively Birgit pulls Karl to her, breaking him free of
Justin's hand. The crossing guard stops, waves her sign
angrily at the motor bike, mothers and children bunching up
behind her, some showing signs of panic...

                                                        (CONTINUED)

82   CONTINUED: (2)

...and as the bike flashes through the gap, the pillion
passenger raises a hand - something clutched in it, something
gleaming, pointing--

-Justin pushing himself in front of Birgit and Karl to shield
them-

-the pillion rider squeezing the bulb of what turns out to be
an old-fashioned motor horn.

BEEP, BEEP

Some of the children laugh.

BIRGIT - white-faced as the crossing continues.

                    JUSTIN (CONT'D)
               Who is Lorbeer?

                    BIRGIT
               A white coat. He invented Dypraxa.
               With Lara Emrich.

ANGLE - A BLACK BMW 760i, parked on the opposite kerb, its
impenetrable windows hiding God-knows-what.

                    JUSTIN
               Where can I find him?

Birgit shakes her head.

                    BIRGIT
               Disappeared.

                    JUSTIN
               Murdered?

                    BIRGIT
               Disappeared.

                    JUSTIN
               And Lara Emrich?

                    BIRGIT
               KDH has her. Quarantined, like a
               disease.

They're almost to the far side now. And the driver's door of
the BMW is slowly opening...

                    JUSTIN
                    (urgently)
               Where?

                                                        (CONTINUED)

No answer. Birgit has turned off the tap.

At the kerb the crowd is dispersing rapidly - some going
right, some left, others ahead.

A BIG MAN in a dark suit is climbing out of the BMW...

Birgit veers off to her bicycle, almost dragging Karl, who is
trying to wave goodbye to Justin.

                    JUSTIN (CONT'D)
               (calling; desperate)
          Where?

Birgit doesn't respond. She's frantically strapping Karl into
his bike harness. Completing the task, she mounts. As she
rides away, she passes Justin...

...leans over and whispers-

                    BIRGIT
          Where they make Dypraxa.

The BMW's CHAUFFEUR has stopped in the roadway to look at
Justin, who is standing at the kerb staring at him, tensed
for action, ready for fight or flight.

Then, with a shake of his head, the man opens the BMW's rear
door...and into the car climbs a MOTHER AND CHILD who have
crossed with Justin's crowd. The chauffeur gets back behind
the wheel. The car glides off.

Justin continues straight ahead.

83   **INT. HALLWAY/JUSTIN'S HOTEL ROOM. DAY**   83

Justin approaches his room along a corridor, unlocks and
pushes open the door. The SOUND of ANGRY CONVERSATION IN
GERMAN, audible in the hallway, becomes suddenly loud.

He hesitates. The room is gloomy, the curtains drawn.
Something isn't right here.

But as he takes a step inside he realizes, with some relief,
that the voices are emanating from his television. Justin
crosses to turn it off---

---and is jumped - so fast, so violently that for moments in
the half-light we're not sure how many attackers there are.

Knees, fists, boots thud into Justin's soft places - the only
live sound in the room his groans and his assailants' effort-
laden breathing. The soap opera continues as background.

                                                    (CONTINUED)

83   CONTINUED:

REVEAL THE FOOTBALL-PLAYING YOUTHS

The flurry of blows and kicks has left Justin curled up on
the carpet, vomiting. One of the three now crouches by him,
wadding up a wash cloth he has taken from the bathroom.

                    YOUTH # 1
          Fertig?

No response. He flicks Justin's face with his fingernail.

                    YOUTH # 1 (CONT'D)
          Finished?

Justin nods. The youth wipes his mouth with the cloth - a
curiously attentive gesture.

Another youth is tying Justin's hands behind his back with
the cord from a dressing gown.

The last attacker lowers the volume on the TV, unfolds a
scrap of lined yellow paper, torn from a legal pad.

                    YOUTH # 2
          (reading)
          "To Justin Quayle, travelling as
          Michael Adams. Stop or you join
          your wife. Last warning."

He thrusts the yellow note in Justin's face.

                    YOUTH # 2 (CONT'D)
          Next time the red card, *ja*?

The other footballers appreciate the joke. One of them kicks
Justin in the groin. As he doubles up, the other two hug the
"goal scorer" and dance around the room in mock-celebration,
chanting the victory chant of German football fans. The
chanting stops at the door. They leave in silence.

Justin is left writhing on the floor, fighting the spasms of
nausea rippling through his body. He lapses into semi-
consciousness for a moment. When he opens his eyes...

ANGLE ON THE OPEN BATHROOM DOOR

Through the doorway we see the same mirror reflection we saw
in Scene 10: Tessa in her underwear at the washbasin.

CLOSE ON JUSTIN'S HANDS as he struggles to free them.

(CONTINUED)

83   CONTINUED: (2)   83

CLOSE ON JUSTIN'S HANDS

now carefully digging up a plant, gently conserving with a
cupped palm the soil around its roots.

84   **INT. FOREIGN & COMMONWEALTH OFFICE, LONDON. DAY**   84

The plant is in a window box outside Justin's office at the
FCO, an office cluttered with packing cases labelled "BRITISH
HIGH COMMISSION, NAIROBI" and a profusion of books about
Kenya.

Turning from the window with the excavated plant, to lay it
alongside others in an insulated travel box ("PLANTS WITH
CARE. DO NOT EXPOSE TO FROST"), Justin finds

TESSA in the 12-foot-high doorway.

                    TESSA
          Take me to Africa with you.

                    JUSTIN
             (smiles)
          Rolled up in a rug.

                    TESSA
          I'm serious.

                    JUSTIN
          Yes, I can see you are.
             (a beat)
          In what capacity am I to take you
          to Africa?

                    TESSA
          I don't mind. Mistress, wife.
             (shrugs)
          Whichever.

Justin smooths back the hair from his forehead, the automatic
gesture he uses when troubled or confused.

                    JUSTIN
          Tessa, naturally I'm flattered...

                    TESSA
          No! Don't even think about
          finishing that sentence. Yes or no?

                    JUSTIN
          We hardly know one another...

                    TESSA
          You can learn me.

                                              (CONTINUED)

84   CONTINUED: 84

Again the hair-sweeping gesture. A moment or two, then:

                         JUSTIN
                    Then...yes.

He seems surprised by his own response, like a man who has
walked into a trap only to discover as he springs it that
it's one he set himself.

                         TESSA
                    You will always protect me, won't
                    you?

                         JUSTIN
                    Of course.

                         TESSA
                    And I you.

BACK TO PRESENT-DAY SCENE

As Justin's hands come free of the bindings-

                         JUSTIN
                    (anguished)
                    Why didn't you tell me? I could
                    have protected you...

ANGLE ON THE BATHROOM MIRROR

Nothing there. Never was.

OVERLAP SOUND NAIROBI METALWORKERS

84A   *EXT. NAIROBI STREET. DAY*   84A

Jomo cycles past the METALWORKERS...

WIDEN SHOT TO

85   *INT. HIGH COMMISSION, NAIROBI. DAY*   85

                         SANDY
                    It is my sad duty to inform you
                    that Dr Bluhm has been found....

A susurrus of response.

86   *EXT. A REMOTE DESERT SPOT, TURKANA. DAY*   86

We see partial images of ARNOLD BLUHM hanging from a tree.

                                                        (CONTINUED)

86   CONTINUED:

                         SANDY (V.O.)
              I'll spare you the details. Suffice
              it to say the poor fellow appears
              to have been tortured to death on
              the same day Tessa was killed....

BACK TO SCENE

                         SANDY (CONT'D)
              Which would seem to exonerate
              him...

                         GHITA
                    (sarcastic)
              Seem, Sandy? What's the new theory?
              Tortured himself to death? Save you
              looking for anyone else?

                         SANDY
                    (ignoring her)
              Moving on....

                                                 CUT TO:

CU A BOUQUET OF FLOWERS MOVING AGAINST A BACKDROP OF SNOW

CU JUSTIN

                         IMMIGRATION OFFICIAL (O.C.)
                    (Canadian accent)
              What is the purpose of your visit
              to Canada?

                         JUSTIN
              Seeing a friend.

A FLOWER DELIVERY VAN TRAVELLING THROUGH SNOW

CU JUSTIN'S PASSPORT

being stamped for entry. The name on it: "ROBERT BLACK".

THE FLOWERS BEING CARRIED INTO A BUILDING

87   *EXT. KDH TOWER - DAWES, SASKATCHEWAN. DAY*   87

This is the only high-rise building in a low-rise prairie
town, set in a thousand-mile snowfield: a gleaming WHITE
STONE MEGALITH with windows of coppered glass opaque to the
world, an unsullied frontage declaring power through purity,
domination through wealth.

                                                 (CONTINUED)

Behind the building rise two clean white chimneys, each with "KDH" lettered in gold down its length, and again that trademark hypodermic steel spire jammed into the cold sky.

The flower delivery van is parked outside.

88   **INT. KDH BUILDING - LOBBY. DAY**   88

The DELIVERY DRIVER is waiting at the front desk with his bouquet and clipboard as LARA EMRICH arrives. She is a tall, handsome woman in her forties, wearing a lab coat.

                    DRIVER
            Dr Emrich?
                (off her nod)
            Sign here.

She signs; he hands her the flowers - all to the amusement of the SECURITY MAN behind the desk.

                    SECURITY MAN
            See, doc? Somebody loves you.

Lara is looking at the card attached to the bouquet. It reads: "UNTIL WE MEET". There's no signature.

REVEAL JUSTIN across the lobby, watching this. His appearance has changed dramatically: a disguise of unkempt hair, stubble, a more casual style of dress. He's standing in front of a TV screen, ostensibly watching a KDH promotional video.

As the film ends - and before it resumes - we hear the KDH musical ID tones and another voice announcing:

                    KDH VOICE (V.O.)
            Karel Delacourt Hudson - the world
            is our clinic.

JUSTIN'S POV - A PUZZLED LARA EMRICH

No idea who sent the flowers or why she had to sign.

The reason is Justin: now he knows what she looks like.

89   **EXT. KDH BUILDING - RAMP. LATE DAY**   89

Lara leaves the building, carrying the bouquet. It has begun to snow. As she crosses the ramp towards the road she finds Justin blocking her way.

                    JUSTIN
            I sent the flowers. My name is
            Justin Quayle.

                                              (CONTINUED)

                                LARA
                    What do you want for them?

                                JUSTIN
                    Nothing. Just to talk to you. About
                    Dypraxa.

        Lara thrusts the bouquet into Justin's hand.

                                LARA
                    I do my job. I don't talk to the
                    press. Why can't you people leave
                    me alone?

90   EXT. KDH - BUS STOP. LATE DAY   90

        It's still snowing as Justin joins Lara in the bus queue.

                                JUSTIN
                    I understand your fear. They've
                    threatened me too.

        He hands back the bouquet. She accepts it.

                                JUSTIN (CONT'D)
                    They killed my wife.

                                LARA
                    You will never find them.

                                JUSTIN
                    I'm not trying to. I just...want to
                    complete her work.

                                LARA
                    Then they will find you. KDH have
                    already murdered me. A year ago I
                    was Head of Research. Now I develop
                    hand cream.

                                JUSTIN
                    What did you do to deserve that?

        A bus arrives, pulling up with a wheeze of air brakes,
        scattering slush. Lara boards. Justin appears not to.

91   INT. BUS (TRAVELLING). LATE DAY   91

        The bus moves off. Lara is sitting alone.

        Justin appears IN SHOT and takes the seat beside her. Neither
        of them speaks as the bus passes through the snowbound
        suburbs of Dawes: scattered houses, driveways both cleared
        and uncleared. Until eventually:

                                                            (CONTINUED)

91   CONTINUED: 91

                              LARA
                    I told the truth.

92   **EXT. BUS/HIGHWAY. LATE DAY**   92

        THE BUS SEEN FROM BEHIND as it rolls through the suburbs.

        ADJUST ANGLE TO REVEAL A CORNER OF A CAR WINDSCREEN - BEHIND
        THE BUS.

                              LARA (V.O.)
                    Dypraxa isn't ready for marketing.
                    The trials were fixed. Whenever we
                    got a side effect - blindness,
                    liver problems - they made us
                    change the rules to exclude these
                    patients.

        BACK TO SCENE

                              LARA (CONT'D)
                    It became very soon the test that
                    could not be failed. When the
                    patients started to die Markus
                    jumped clear. Or was pushed.

                              JUSTIN
                    Markus is Lorbeer?

                              LARA
                    Yes. We conducted the trials in
                    Kenya. For ThreeBees - they had the
                    franchise.

                              JUSTIN
                    Why ThreeBees?

        She shrugs. Doesn't know, doesn't care.

                              JUSTIN (CONT'D)
                    How many patients died?

                              LARA
                    Officially, none. If someone died
                    their name was removed, the body
                    was removed. When I left, forty-
                    one.

                              JUSTIN
                    And nobody protested?

                              LARA
                    I protested. So they scream about
                    my confidentiality agreement.
                              (MORE)

                                                        (CONTINUED)

92   CONTINUED: 92

                        LARA (CONT'D)
              If I shut up they will give me a
              job - here, in Canada. A house, a
              visa, everything. If I don't they
              will destroy me.

                        JUSTIN
              Lorbeer didn't back you?

                        LARA
                   (grim laugh)
              Where is Judas when you need him?

                        JUSTIN
              I think you know where he is.

93   **EXT. BUS/SUBURBAN ROAD. DAY**   93

    The bus comes to a halt. Lara climbs down. Justin follows.
    The bus moves on.

    Across the highway, through the whirling snowflakes, we can
    see Lara's house, set back some way from the road, its
    driveway unswept. There's no traffic here. They cross the
    road.

                        LARA
              This is where I live. You should go
              back to town before the storm gets
              worse.

                        JUSTIN
              What does Lorbeer look like?

    She stops, puzzled by the question.

                        JUSTIN (CONT'D)
              I think I may have seen him.

                        LARA
              Markus looks like a man, but has
              the soul of a reptile. Now you
              will ask how could a woman love
              such a thing?

    She moves on across the road. Justin catches up with her at
    the verge, almost at the entrance to her driveway.

                        JUSTIN
              That I wouldn't presume to
              question. I won't harm him, Lara.
              You have my word.

    She stops again.

                                              (CONTINUED)

                         LARA
          It will make no difference to
          expose these people, Justin. They
          are immune.

                         JUSTIN
          You fought them - once.

                         LARA
          Yes. I lost.

Silence.

                         JUSTIN
          Where is he, Lara?

                         LARA
          Be careful what you wish for.
          Markus is married to his Christian
          conscience, but he cheats on her.
          He betrays, he repents, he is
          cleansed to sin again. If you find
          him he will betray you too.

                         JUSTIN
          I'll take that risk.

                         LARA
                (a sigh; her resistance
                eroded)
          Ten days ago he writes me about a
          report someone has given him - on
          the Kenya trials. "Dear Lara, I
          have betrayed everyone. Now I do my
          penance in the wilderness." This
          with half the Bible to support it.

                         JUSTIN
          Did he say where he was?

By way of answer she opens her purse, takes from it a folded
DHL envelope, thrusts it into Justin's hand. Attached to the
envelope is a waybill.

INSERT WAYBILL: **"ORIGIN OF CONSIGNMENT: LOKI, KENYA   SENDER:
J. ANDIKA**"

                         JUSTIN (CONT'D)
          Loki.

While Justin is looking at the envelope we're hearing a
succession of LIGHT HISSING SOUNDS; pockmarks appear in the
snow.

Justin looks up to see Lara falling, struck by a bullet from
a silenced rifle. The bouquet lands beside her in the snow.

He stoops to help her but sees immediately that she is dead.
He looks around for the assassin, but none is identifiable -
just an ELDERLY MAN shovelling snow from the doorway of a
house, a car parked some distance away in the opposite
direction, a tractor in a field, a truck passing on the
highway...

The HISS OF FURTHER BULLETS striking the snow around him
urges Justin into action. He runs towards the ELDERLY MAN,
who has seen Lara lying in the snow and has stopped his
shovelling to advance towards the body. OTHER NEIGHBOURS have
seen the event too and are coming to investigate.

The car starts up and moves off...

ON JUSTIN, running off into the growing blizzard, his face a
mask of anguish and guilt as it dawns on him that he, not
Lara, was the assassin's target; and that just by being with
her he got her killed.

94   *EXT. WOODROWS' GARDEN (UNDER AWNING) - NAIROBI. NIGHT*   94

Here, contrastingly, it's a hot equatorial evening. At
Sandy's promotion dinner some ten or a dozen High Commission
people are seated at a long table under a bright awning. We
recognize SANDY, GLORIA, DONOHUE, GHITA, MILDREN and MIRIAM
but there are others we don't know, including MAUD DONOHUE.

Jomo is collecting the dirty soup plates.

                    MILDREN
          Sandy, I've a question. Now you're
          confirmed as High Commissioner, do
          we still have to be polite to Kenny
          Curtiss?

Laughter at this from all but Donohue.

                    SANDY
          Theoretical question, Mike. I doubt
          he'll be around much longer.
               (catching Donohue's eye)
          Anyone seen ThreeBees share price
          lately?
               (signs spiralling fall)

95   *INT. KITCHEN. NIGHT*   95

Inside, the heat is infernal, the cook dripping sweat.

                                                        (CONTINUED)

Jomo enters, dumps his tray and picks up a tray of entrees.
There's a folded note tucked between two of the plates.

                    MUSTAFA
                (in Swahili)
        The note is for Mr Woodrow.

Jomo nods, then makes to go. Mustafa stops him.

                    MUSTAFA (CONT'D)
        How have you been?

Jomo shrugs.

                    MUSTAFA (CONT'D)
        Are you taking any medicine? There
        are treatments you can get for it.

                    JOMO
        Yes, for 60 U.S. dollars a month
        you can treat it. Plus a hundred
        for viral load and another thirty
        for CD4 count.
                (wry smile)
        More than I earn.

                    MUSTAFA
        Don't give up hope, my friend.

Jomo shakes his head, but whether it signifies lack of hope
or refusal to give up hope isn't clear. He pushes out through
the door.

96   **EXT. DINNER PARTY. NIGHT**   96

                    DONOHUE
        Hardly Kenny's fault if someone put
        the word out on him.

                    MILDREN
        Wish I'd known that's all it took.
        I'd have done it sooner.

Laughter.

                    SANDY
                (looking at Donohue)
        I expect he'll land on his feet.
        They'll give him a life peerage.

                    GLORIA
                 (H.M. voice)
          "Henceforth you shall be known as:
          'Lord Fucking Curtiss of Fucking
          Kenya'."

During the prolonged laughter at this *bon mot,* Jomo delivers
the note to Sandy. Sandy scans it.

Ghita watching him.

                    SANDY
                 (to dinner guests)
          Excuse me a moment.

ANGLE ON DONOHUE watching as Sandy goes into the garden.

ANGLE ON GARDEN - a spot where the fence is overgrown with
shrubbery.

SANDY'S POV: AN UNIDENTIFIED FIGURE IN THE SHADOWS

seen from behind, snapping dead growth from a hibiscus.

                    SANDY (CONT'D)
          Whoever you are, I don't take
          kindly to being blackmailed...

The figure turns...

REVEAL JUSTIN

                    SANDY (CONT'D)
                 (taken aback)
          Christ! How did you get here?

                    JUSTIN
          Canadian safari tour. Via Paris.

                    SANDY
          Hunting me now, Justin? You're the
          one on the run.

Justin flourishes the letter. Sandy recognises the blue HMSO
stationery, his trademark.

                    SANDY (CONT'D)
          I loved her. I'm not ashamed of it.

                    JUSTIN
          Nor should you be. If it were true.

                                              (CONTINUED)

                              SANDY
                        (bridling)
                  Not for you to say how I felt.
                  If you've read that you'll know I
                  let her see...something she
                  shouldn't.

                              JUSTIN
                  A letter. Written by Pellegrin.
                  What was in it, Sandy?

                              SANDY
                  What letter would that be?

                              JUSTIN
                  The one everyone's looking for. The
                  one Tessa took.

                              SANDY
                  We don't know who's got that.

                              JUSTIN
                  What did it say?

Sandy shakes his head. Sooner have Gloria see his love letter
than reveal to Justin the contents of Pellegrin's.

                              JUSTIN (CONT'D)
                  And the report she brought you?
                        (off Sandy's silence)
                  She trusted you. You ignored it.

                              SANDY
                  I didn't ignore it, I sent it on in
                  the pouch. London ignored it.
                        (indicating the letter)
                  What do you want for that?

                              JUSTIN
                  I want to know why Pellegrin
                  suppressed Tessa's report. Was him,
                  wasn't it?

                              SANDY
                  Don't try and play detective.

                              JUSTIN
                  ThreeBees - KDH - Dypraxa. What's
                  the story on that axis of evil? KDH
                  is Swiss-Canadian, Dypraxa was
                  invented by a South African and a
                  Scandinavian. Why are we involved?

                        SANDY
            Because Kenny's one of us. He's
            British.
                (outburst)
            Christ, Justin, stop bleeding for
            bloody Africa and show some
            loyalty. Those patients were going
            to die anyway. Would you rather a
            Swiss firm did the testing? Or a
            French one?
            It's a harsh commercial world, man.
            People like you and Porter don't
            understand it.

INSERT REPRISE:

ANGLE ON GARDEN ROOM, where Pellegrin, Coleridge, McKenzie,
Curtiss and Ngaba - an exclusive caucus of five - are
drinking champagne, smoking cigars and talking business.

Justin watches as Sandy is taken through the French doors by
Crick to join them.

                        SANDY(CONT'D)
            That plant KDH built in Wales
            could've gone to France. Fifteen
            hundred jobs, in a depressed
            region. We owed them. They needed
            help with the Kenyan authorities.
            They needed an investment partner
            here for the Dypraxa trials...
                (a shrug)
            Curtiss provided both. Curtiss was
            our quid pro quo.

Justin nods. Understands it now.

                        JUSTIN
            And Tessa wanted what?

                        SANDY
            Pressure on Kenny. Stop the tests,
            re-design the bloody drug. Two
            years' delay...

                        JUSTIN
            Or?

Sandy shakes his head. Suddenly he starts to cry. Justin
waits as he pulls out a handkerchief and blows his nose.

                        SANDY
            We betrayed her. We all did. You
            did it by growing flowers...

                                        (CONTINUED)

96   CONTINUED: (4)

                         JUSTIN
              How did you betray her?

                         SANDY
              They wanted to know what she was up
              to.... I'm the one told them she
              was going up to Loki....

He breaks into tears again.

                         JUSTIN
              Who did you tell?

                         SANDY
              Pellegrin.
                   (a beat, headshake)
              God knows who he told.

Justin steps forward. For an instant it seems he is about to
strike Sandy, but instead he tucks the folded letter into
Sandy's pocket.

Sandy turns and stumbles back towards the party, hunched over
like the victim of a whipping.

97   **EXT. MUTHAIGA STREET. NIGHT**   97

GHITA'S CAR is waiting at the kerb, engine running Ghita at
the wheel ...

... as Justin appears through the service gate in the
boundary fence. He's about to climb into the car when his
attention is taken by ...

A BLACK LIMO kerb-crawling towards him ...

Having already got Lara Emrich killed, Justin isn't about to
risk Ghita's life. He bangs on the roof of her car.

                         JUSTIN
                 Go! Go now!

A moment's hesitation, then Ghita responds. Grinds the car
into gear and takes off.

The limo glides alongside Justin. The tinted front passenger
window slides down

REVEALING KENNY CURTISS beside an AFRICAN DRIVER.

                         CURTISS
                 Get in.

Justin remains where he is, calculating his escape options.

                                              (CONTINUED)

97   CONTINUED: 97

                    CURTISS (CONT'D)
If I wanted you dead I'd have Crick
with me. Get in. I want to show
you something.

                    JUSTIN
Show me from there.

                    CURTISS
Don't mess me about. I'm doing you
a favour.

Justin hesitates. It's a risk, but something in Kenny's tone
tells him it's a risk worth taking. He opens the door and
climbs into the limo's back seat. The car moves off.

98   *INT. CURTISS'S LIMO (TRAVELLING). NIGHT*   98

                    JUSTIN
How did you know where I'd be?

                    CURTISS
I've still got a friend or two.
        (pause)
We're marked men, Quayle. They've
called in my fucking bank loans.
I'm finished. They want you *shtum*
and they want a foreign flag flying
over my pharma division. Let's give
the bastards trouble.

99   *EXT. NAIROBI RIVERSIDE AREA. NIGHT*   99

A desolate stretch of river margin south of the city, near
Kibera: a muddy acre too marshy even to support shanties.

The car stops. Curtiss's tinted window slides open. He
directs a flashlight beam out at the swampy ground.

                    CURTISS
You've been asking about Wanza
Kilulu. She's under there, covered
in quicklime. Her and sixty-two
others.

                    JUSTIN
Dypraxa deaths.

Curtiss nods.

                    JUSTIN (CONT'D)
That where I'm going?

                    CURTISS
         Not on my agenda.

                    JUSTIN
         So why are you showing me this?

                    CURTISS
         Let's just say if I'm going to the
         wall, I want a trophy. What you lot
         do, innit? Heads on walls. Think
         I'll have Head of fucking Africa
         Desk on mine.
               (gesturing)
         Remember where it is. And I'm not
         taking questions.

The window slides closed. He sets the car in motion.

100   **EXT. COUNTRY NORTH OF NAIROBI. EARLY MORNING**   100

POV ANGLE ON TREES seen from a moving car.

REVEAL GHITA'S CAR, Justin driving on a lonely road north
through the Rift Valley.

101   **INT. GHITA'S CAR/MIRROR SHOT.**   101

In his mirror Justin sees that there is a single vehicle some
way behind him, closing fast, HONKING its HORN. It is
discernible through the dust shroud as a Land Rover, colour
indeterminate, two indistinguishable figures inside.

He speeds up. But the Land Rover continues to gain on him.

102   **EXT. THE CHASE.   ROAD/DIRT TRACK**   102

For miles in either direction there is nothing on the road
but the car and the Land Rover as Justin attempts to outrun
his pursuers. He turns left on to a dirt road. Some MASAI
HERDSMEN are herding cattle near the junction.

It's a hopelessly one-sided contest. Ghita's car is old and
underpowered. The Land Rover is built for such country.

AERIAL SHOT - the cars are climbing a cliff, their separate
dust plumes swirling like smoke into the deep blue early
morning sky.

The Land Rover is flashing its lights and sounding its horn
but Justin refuses to stop.

Suddenly the road ends abruptly at the cliff edge. Nowhere
left for Justin to go. He slides to a halt.

103   **INT. CAR - JUSTIN'S POV**   103

The Land Rover's door opens. Justin looks up into the face of
his putative assassin...

REVEAL DONOHUE

JUSTIN'S REACTION - surprise and confusion. Was Tim Donohue
one of the two white men seen buying beer at Kolowa?

> DONOHUE
> Who did you think it was?

> JUSTIN
> Isn't this bandit country?

104   **EXT. CLIFF EDGE - RIFT VALLEY. EARLY MORNING**   104

Donohue's AFRICAN DRIVER is sitting in the Land Rover,
sucking an orange and listening to the radio. Donohue and
Justin are talking by the side of the track.

> JUSTIN
> Did you tell Curtiss where I'd be?

Donohue smiles.

> JUSTIN (CONT'D)
> Ghita's my only friend here. I
> wouldn't want to get her in
> trouble.

> DONOHUE
> She won't be. You've another
> friend, believe it or not.
>   (gesturing)
> Heading for Loki are you?

Justin makes no response. Donohue smiles.

> DONOHUE (CONT'D)
> What you're looking for isn't at
> Loki. Let's be honest with one
> another, shall we.

> JUSTIN
> Late career change for you Tim.

> DONOHUE
> We've something in common, you and
> I. We'll both be dead by Christmas.
> There's a contract out on you -
> same people that did Tessa, I
> shouldn't wonder. Mine's cancer. My
> pain's controllable.

(CONTINUED)

                              JUSTIN
                    I knew you were ill, I didn't...

                              DONOHUE
                    Know I'd booked my retirement
                    cruise on the Titanic?
                         (a beat)
                    Sandy tell you he fingered Tessa?

                              JUSTIN
                    He told me he made a phone call.

                              DONOHUE
                    He didn't know they'd kill her.
                    Silly sod was besotted with her.
                    But that's how it works with
                    corporate murder. Somebody
                    complains to the boss...

INSERT: PELLEGRIN (UNIDENTIFIED) making a phone call from HIS
CLUB.

                         DONOHUE (V.O.) (CONT'D)
                      Boss calls in his head of
                      security...

INSERT: McKENZIE (UNIDENTIFIED) in HIS OFFICE talking to his
HEAD OF SECURITY.

          MCKENZIE   DONOHUE
     (Canadian accent)   He talks to someone...
    We've got a problem...

INSERT: KDH HEAD OF SECURITY making a phone call from another
OFFICE.

      KDH HEAD OF SECURITY   DONOHUE
    That friend of yours, did the ...who talks to a friend of
    other job...   someone...

INSERT: CRICK (UNIDENTIFIED) having a conversation with a
KENYAN POLICEMAN in a CAR PARK, their two cars parked side by
side.

           CRICK   DONOHUE
    Same deal, same terms as last Ends up with an answering
    time...   machine in a rented office...

INSERT: AN EMPTY CITY OFFICE, an answering machine with its
light blinking, recording a message:

104   CONTINUED: (2)

          KENYAN POLICEMAN'S VOICE   DONOHUE
                (V.O.)   ...a couple of mercenaries in
     I'll leave the details to   a green safari truck.
     you. Just get it done...

INSERT: WIDE ANGLE SHOT OF THE MERCENARIES AND THEIR TRUCK AT
MARSABIT

               DONOHUE (CONT'D)
          You'll never know who ordered the
          hit.

                    JUSTIN
          Was it Pellegrin?

                    DONOHUE
          Pellegrin!
               (laughs)
          He'd sooner order his lunch at
          McDonalds.
               (earnestly)
          I can get you out of Kenya. That's
          one of the things we still do well.
          Go home and live your threescore
          and ten, or whatever that is
          inflation-adjusted. I'd give a lot
          for the option.

                    JUSTIN
          I don't have a home. Tessa was my
          home.

                    DONOHUE
          Then I'll see to it you're buried
          with her at Langata.

There's a pause. A BOY herding goats crosses the road in
front of them.

               DONOHUE (CONT'D)
          Know about Bluhm?
               (off Justin's nod)
          Let me tell you what you're facing.

INSERT: the remains of ARNOLD BLUHM, ravaged in life by the
cruellest tortures and *post mortem* by wild beasts, are being
taken down by KENYAN POLICEMEN from the tree on which he was
crucified.

               DONOHUE (CONT'D)
          They dragged him out into the
          desert, cut out his tongue, chopped
          off his manly apparatus, stuffed it
          where the tongue had been.
               (MORE)

                                                    (CONTINUED)

104   CONTINUED: (3)   104

                    DONOHUE (CONT'D)
            Then they crucified the poor
            bugger. Pathologist's opinion is he
            was alive when they nailed him up.

                    JUSTIN
            It's not an end I'd choose.

                    DONOHUE
            You might get lucky. Could be in
            their interest to make yours look
            like suicide - which it is. Balance
            of the mind disturbed. No enquiry,
            no scandal. Less messy all round.

                    JUSTIN
            Thank you for warning me. You've
            been very kind.

Donohue reaches inside his shirt and pulls out a 9mm
automatic pistol. For the briefest of moments we might think,
with Justin, that Donohue has come to kill him after all. But
he hands the pistol to Justin, butt first.

                    DONOHUE
            In case you meet any bandits.

104A   *INT. CAR. DAY*   104A

We see on the seat beside Justin the gun and the envelope
given to him in Canada by Lara.

                                TILT UP TO
                                REVEAL:

104B   *EXT. LOKI STREETS. DAY*   104B

105   *EXT. LOKI AIRSTRIP. DAY*   105

An ancient Buffalo aircraft is loading supplies for a food
drop in Sudan. Justin can be seen talking to its Kenyan
pilot, JONAH ANDIKA.

106   *EXT. KENYA-SUDAN BORDERLANDS- AERIAL SHOT. DAY* 106

We're looking down from the same Buffalo at 6,000 feet: at
the divide where the dun-coloured wastes of Northern Kenya
merge with the emerald swamplands of south-eastern Sudan,
these misted by heat and pierced with jigsaw-shaped black
holes of water.

107   *INT. BUFFALO. DAY*   107

The POV is JUSTIN'S. A headset over his ears, he's watching
the landscape from a Victorian armchair clamped to the floor
in the nose of the aircraft, just behind the open cockpit.

                                        (CONTINUED)

CONTINUED:

The courier envelope Lorbeer sent to Lara is in his hand:
"SENDER: J. ANDIKA, LOKI".

                    JUSTIN
          Thank you for agreeing to take me,
          Mr Andika.

                    JONAH
          Jonah. No formality up here.
               (a beat)
          I got plenty of room on the dinner
          run. Do it four times a day.

ANGLE THROUGH WINDOW as the plane begins its descent.

JUSTIN'S POV - THE PLANE'S REFLECTION, which appears golden
above the marshes. The ground colours merging into mist.

The swamp turns brown and single trees appear, green like
cauliflowers in the bright anti-shadow of the sunlit plane.

ANGLE - AID WORKERS releasing food sacks, bag after bag
sliding from the rack like a benign bombing raid...

                    JONAH (CONT'D)
          Longest emergency airlift in
          history.

                    JUSTIN
          Why don't they take it in by road?
          Cheaper, surely.

                    JONAH
          There's more paved road in your
          driveway than in the whole of South
          Sudan.

108   *EXT. VILLAGE. DAY*   108

A white cross has been marked out on the ground, the food
bags landing on and around it in a haze of dust. A queue of
VILLAGERS waits for distribution to be authorised by the TWO
WORLD FOOD PROGRAM REPS there for the purpose.

109   *INT. BUFFALO. DAY*   109

                    JONAH
          This is a country that shouldn't
          exist. Another one of those nations
          invented by colonial map-makers.
               (MORE)

                        JONAH (CONT'D)
          You throw together an extremist
          Arab Moslem government in the
          North, Africans sitting on oil
          fields in the South, and you get a
          fine little twenty-year war that
          was going on here 'til about five
          minutes ago. Two million dead. Oil
          doesn't mix with water, but it
          mixes fine with blood.

                        JUSTIN
          What happened five minutes ago?

                        JONAH
          The international oil companies got
          tired of waiting for peace to break
          out. Those fellows like to drill
          without getting their heads blown
          off, you know. They leaned on
          America to stop the fighting - that
          plus moral pressure from the
          Christian Right. Everyday African
          story. Better strap yourself in.
          We're landing on the surface of the
          moon.

Justin buckles his seat belt. Items of cargo shift as the
aircraft banks steeply and a cluster of conical rush-roofed
huts bursts into view beyond its wing tip. We glimpse a
reception committee: LOCAL DIGNITARIES, AID WORKERS,
CHILDREN, DINKA PORTERS - all waiting in the intense heat.

110   **EXT. CAMP SEVEN AIRSTRIP, SOUTHERN SUDAN. DAY**   110

The airstrip is surfaced with red dust and partly overgrown.
Clouds of dust flame into the air as the ancient Buffalo
lands, shuddering, its engines screaming. Finally it comes to
rest; the engines die, the dust slowly subsides...

...and like a vision generated out of dust particles and heat
shimmer, a wraith in khaki shorts and a brown Homburg
resolves itself slowly into flesh at the runway's edge...

...MARKUS LORBEER

JUSTIN REACTS. The "doctor" he saw attending Wanza Kilulu.

                        JONAH (V.O.)
          That's Brandt. Works at the local
          clinic. He's a born-again
          Christian. Don't get him started.

111   **EXT. AIRSTRIP/FOOD CAMP. DAY**   111

The Buffalo is being unloaded under the supervision of GARAN,
the Food Monitor. TOPOSA WOMEN, each with a numbered ticket,
are in line to collect the food sacks. Some are bare-
breasted, others sheathed in copper-coloured cloth or white
synthetic sacking. Hoisting the bags onto their heads, they
begin the return to their village, elegant as models on a
catwalk.

Garan separates out the medical equipment for "Brandt"
(LORBEER) to take away. Lorbeer has not recognised Justin as
the man he once saw half-turned away on Tessa's bed in Uhuru.

A ten-year-old Sudanese boy, whom we will know only as
"NEMO", is helping Lorbeer with the boxes.

> JUSTIN
> (introducing himself)
> Robert Black. Freelance journalist.
> They tell me you're the man to talk
> to, Dr Brandt.

> LORBEER
> I don't know about that. But I can
> tell you how things are here.
> (shouting to Nemo)
> I'll leave the unloading in your
> capable hands, Nemo.
> (to Justin)
> My self-appointed assistant.

> NEMO
> (to Justin; his only
> English sentence)
> How are you?

> JUSTIN
> Very well, thank you.

Justin and Lorbeer start to walk towards the camp.

111A   **EXT. HILL TOP. DAY**   111A

Justin and Lorbeer are walking towards the medical area.

> LORBEER
> They only give food to the women.
> The women make the homes. All the
> men make is wars and hooch. Adam
> was God's first draft, Robert. He
> got it right with Eve. Tell that to
> your readers.

(CONTINUED)

JUSTIN
It's a philosophy I learned from my
wife.

Lorbeer looks at him. A hint of recognition? Something...

LORBEER
Cherish her, man. She is God's
finest work. Now I'll show you what
the Devil is up to.

112   **EXT. CAMP MEDICAL AREA. DAY**   112

Nemo and a number of ADULT PORTERS are carrying boxes of
medical equipment to where a line of sheds marks the hospital
area. A sign reads "MISSION OF CHRIST THE HEALER".

To each shed is attached an enclosure crammed with the
desperately sick. Battle-weary PARAMEDICS and AID AGENCY
DOCTORS move among them, mustering them into an order for
treatment.

LORBEER
(to Justin)
Our treatment centre. Crude, hey?

Lorbeer pries open one of the crates to check its contents.

JUSTIN
I've seen hospitals little better.
(a beat)
In Nairobi.

LORBEER
So have I.

He starts to rummage through the contents, rapidly reading
brand names and sell-by dates on the drug cartons. Some he
leaves in the crate, others he stacks beside it.

LORBEER (CONT'D)
Ex-factory medicines, past their
use-by. The drug companies donate
them. It's a tax break for them -
disposable drugs for disposable
patients. Dissolve two in the milk
of human kindness, take with food
if you have any.

TWO DISPENSARY ASSISTANTS appear. Lorbeer indicates the
discard pile. The assistants pick up the cartons and begin to
carry them off to an oil drum from which smoke is rising.

(CONTINUED)

112   CONTINUED:

                          LORBEER (CONT'D)
              Out here they have no shelf life.
              The safest thing to do with them is
              incinerate them.
              The pharmaceutical companies are
              right up there with the arms
              dealers. This is how the world
              fucks Africa.

                          JUSTIN
              Blood on their hands, Brandt?

                          LORBEER
                   (a broad gesture)
              This is how they expiate their
              guilt. Big Pharma, the aid
              agencies, everybody. This machine
              is driven by guilt.

He puts his arm around Justin's shoulder.

                          LORBEER (CONT'D)
              Now you sample our goat stew.

112A   *EXT. CAMP. DAY*   112A

Justin and Lorbeer pass various groups of VILLAGERS who,
having no clear function or purpose, simply stand around
looking lost. (Sebastian Selgados images)

113   *INT. LORBEER'S TUKUL. DAY*   113

The spartan interior contains a table made of wooden pallets,
beer cases for seats, a single hard chair (under it a
backpack), a stove. Lorbeer is occupying the chair, Justin a
crate. Nemo is sitting on the floor. All three are eating
stew from enamel mugs.

                          LORBEER
              Do you believe an individual can
              redeem himself by good acts?

                          JUSTIN
              Yes.

                          LORBEER
              Maybe the redemption is in the
              struggle. God has your head, the
              Devil has your balls.

                          JUSTIN
              Which devil had yours?

                                                        (CONTINUED)

113   CONTINUED:

> LORBEER
> You don't want to know about that.
> What's your paper interested in?

> JUSTIN
> The pharmaceutical multis. African
> guinea pigs. Cheap clinical trials
> for unsound drugs. Uninformed
> consent extorted with threats
> against children. Pay-offs. Cover-
> ups. Unmarked graves. Murder.

Lorbeer has begun to sweat heavily. Rising from his chair, he
commences to prowl the *tukul:* a hunted man confronted by a
chasm.

> LORBEER
> Who are you?

> JUSTIN
> Don't you know?

Lorbeer has pressed his body to the wall, as though bracing
himself for torture. He raises his head to Heaven.

> LORBEER
> God Christ, you were at the
> hospital. I knew I'd seen you
> somewhere. You're the husband.

> JUSTIN
> And you are Markus Lorbeer.

114   **EXT. FOOD CAMP. DAY**   114

WIDE SHOT from medical centre. Something out here is
disturbing the food station's tranquillity. People and cattle
are on the move - not yet in panic but heading out of the
station into the bush.

Dust thrown up by horses is visible on the distant horizon.

POV changes to LORBEER: seeing this through the open door
flap of the tukul.

115   **INT. TUKUL. DAY**   115

> LORBEER
> There's something going on out
> there.

> JUSTIN
> Why did my wife come here?

                         LORBEER
               They had this report they'd
               written. Inspired guesswork. I was
               supposed to provide the missing
               clinical data. Testify on tape.

                         JUSTIN
               Did you?

Half Lorbeer's attention is elsewhere - on what's going on
outside the tukul.

In the distance WE SEE Jonah speaking to Garan, who breaks
away and starts to run towards the medical area. AID WORKERS,
in white t-shirts, are running towards the plane.

                         LORBEER
               Could be a raid. Tribesmen. They
               steal food, cattle, children.

                         JUSTIN
               Did you?

                         LORBEER
               She was a persuasive woman, your
               wife. I don't have the tape. They
               took it with them.

                         JUSTIN
               But you kept the report?

                         LORBEER
               You're welcome to it.

He rummages in his backpack, finds and thrusts into Justin's
hands a manila envelope, from which Justin takes a typed
document held together by a staple.

As Justin leafs through it, Garan appears in the doorway.
He's in a hurry, stopping only long enough to say:

                         GARAN
               Level 4 alert. The plane is going
               in five minutes.

Lorbeer grabs his backpack, hurriedly straps it on.

                         LORBEER
               You don't want to die, my friend,
               you better come with me to that
               airstrip.

116   **EXT. CAMP. DAY**   116

Lorbeer, Justin and Nemo have emerged from the tukul. Dust
thrown up by horses is visible on the distant horizon.

In the main camp area, all around them, women are gathering
their children, preparing to flee. One of them takes Nemo's
hand and leads him away. It should be apparent that if they
run hard, Lorbeer and Justin will still make it to the plane
in time. Its engines have begun to turn over.

                    LORBEER
          We can still make it-

But as he sets himself to make the dash to the airstrip
Justin suddenly holds him fast.

                    JUSTIN
          What were Tessa and Bluhm doing at
          Lake Turkana?

                    LORBEER
          You crazy? We've got to get out.
          Those people'll kill anyone.

                    JUSTIN
          Not until you've told me what I
          want to know.

Lorbeer attempts to pull free of Justin's grip, but Justin
isn't letting go.

Around them, VILLAGE MEN, having grabbed whatever weapons
they can lay their hands on, are going out to engage the
raiders, passing fleeing women and children.

                    LORBEER
          They were on their way to Marsabit.
          Taking the whole rotten package to
          Grace Makanga. She'd have put it in
          front of the U.N. They'd missed her
          in Loki. Turkana was as far as they
          got.

They look towards the airstrip and see that HORSEMEN are
already between the village and the plane.

                    JUSTIN
               (waving the report)
          This isn't all she brought you.
          There was something else, wasn't
          there? A letter.

                                              (CONTINUED)

A flicker of response from Lorbeer tells Justin he's hit the mark.

>   LORBEER
>   For God's sake, man!

116A   **EXT. CAMP. DAY**   116A

VARIOUS ANGLES

A BOY running to warn the camp.

RAIDERS close behind him.

The RAIDERS reach the village.

WE SEE

VILLAGERS killed,

GIRLS being kidnapped,

VILLAGE MEN fighting back...

116B   **EXT. AIRSTRIP. DAY**   116B

The last of the Aid Workers are boarding the plane. Jonah closes the Buffalo's door, sealing off that safe haven.

116C   **EXT. CAMP. DAY**   116C

Gripping Lorbeer's arm, Justin starts to run in the direction the villagers are taking, pulling Lorbeer with him.

>   LORBEER
>   You lunatic! You know what you've
>   done? You've killed us both.

>   JUSTIN
>   (indicating the fleeing
>   villagers)
>   We'll take our chances with them.

ANGLE - OLD MEN, WOMEN, CHILDREN, CATTLE surging towards a concealed valley in the dusty ground, a fertile oasis.

ANGLE - FOUR BURNING HUTS.

A group of raiders are pursuing some women around the huts. A second group of raiders, riding in the opposite direction, cuts off their escape.

116D   *EXT. EDGE OF OASIS. DAY*   116D

ANGLE ON LORBEER

as he finally shrugs himself free of Justin...

ANGLE ON A HORSEMAN, shooting off his rifle---

---as JUSTIN dives on Lorbeer, pulling him to the ground.

The bullet which misses Lorbeer strikes the woman who tried
to help them. She falls without a sound.

JUSTIN'S REACTION: aware that if he hadn't cleared the
bullet's path by saving Lorbeer she would not have been hit.

Having seen the incident, Nemo turns back to lead Justin and
Lorbeer to safety.

116E   *EXT. CAMP. DAY*   116E

SIX CHILDREN, running from the village, are followed by
HORSEMEN and rounded up.

119   *EXT. OASIS. DAY*   119

VILLAGERS and CATTLE have moved into an oasis area, which
they now inhabit like ghosts, moving silently among the lush
vegetation. The oasis curves around the village back towards
the airstrip. Between the palms smoke can be glimpsed rising
from burning huts.

Nemo beside him, Lorbeer hunkers down in the relative safety
of the oasis; mops his face with a kerchief.

                    LORBEER
                  (to Justin)
          Thanks. For what you did.

                    JUSTIN
          I don't want your thanks. I want
          what I came for.

                    LORBEER
          They would have made that tape
          public. Don't mistake me. I don't
          care about my life. But they would
          have stopped my work. The work is
          what matters.

                    JUSTIN
          How did they know where to find
          her?

                                              (CONTINUED)

119   CONTINUED: 119

                              LORBEER
                    What?

                              JUSTIN
                    My wife. How did they know where
                    she'd be?

          A long pause.

                              LORBEER
                    I radioed Nairobi. KDH's security
                    guy, name of Crick. Christ, man, I
                    didn't know they'd be murdered. My
                    oath to God.

                              JUSTIN
                    I want that letter.

          After a moment of hesitation, Lorbeer unstraps a pocket in
          his backpack and pulls out a Bible. From inside it he
          withdraws a folded letter. Hands this to Justin.

                              LORBEER
                    That was my insurance policy.

          Justin unfolds the letter and scans it.

                              LORBEER (CONT'D)
                    Life is simple here, Quayle.
                         (gestures)
                    Death or survival. We don't fret
                    about whose flag gets spattered
                    when the shit hits the fan.

120   **EXT. CAMP SEVEN AIRSTRIP/OASIS. DAY**   120

          Nemo has accompanied Justin and Lorbeer to the point where
          the oasis abuts the airstrip. The plane has started to taxi.

                              NEMO
                         (in Turkana, pointing)
                    *Let's run to the plane. They can't
                    see us from here.*

120A   **EXT. BUFFALO. DAY**   120A

          JONAH'S POV FROM COCKPIT:

          THE THREE FIGURES running ahead of the plane.

120B   **EXT/INT. BUFFALO. DAY**   120B

          The plane has stopped. The door has been opened. Justin,
          Lorbeer and Nemo clamber aboard.

                                                        (CONTINUED)

Jonah has left the cockpit and is barring the door.

> JONAH
> I can't take the boy.

> JUSTIN
> I'm not leaving him.

> JONAH
> I understand your feelings, Justin.
> We're only allowed to evacuate the
> aid workers.

> JUSTIN
> To hell with what's allowed.

Jonah shrugs. Nothing he can do.

Justin pulls out of his pocket a fistful of cash.

> JUSTIN (CONT'D)
> How much to take him?

> JONAH
> You can't buy this. The rules are
> there for a reason.

> JUSTIN
> This is a child's life. There
> aren't any rules to cover that.

> JONAH
> There are thousands of them. I
> can't make an exception for one
> child.

> JUSTIN
> (an echo of Tessa's words)
> This one's here. Now. This is one
> we can help.

He looks around for Nemo, but Nemo has gone.

Jonah lays a sympathetic hand on Justin's shoulder.

> JONAH
> Do you think I haven't been here
> before?

Jonah returns to the cockpit.

JUSTIN'S POV: NEMO

Heading back into the oasis. Not wanting to be fought over.

(CONTINUED)

120B   CONTINUED: (2)   120B

                              JUSTIN
                         (to Lorbeer)
                    What will happen to him.

                              LORBEER
                    A refugee camp.
                         (a beat)
                    If he's lucky.

In the crowded fuselage Justin seats himself next to Lorbeer
while Jonah resumes taxi-ing. Through the window he is still
watching - an echo of scene 20 - the small figure of Nemo
disappearing into the foliage.

A moment or two of silence, then:

                              LORBEER (CONT'D)
                    Crick's going to know you were up
                    here. He'll ask where you were
                    headed. What do I tell him?

                              JUSTIN
                    He'll know. He's been there before.

120C   **INT. BUFFALO. DAY**   120C

Justin stands up and walks towards the cockpit.

ANGLE ON Justin talking in Jonah's ear, showing him the map
printed out from the Grace Makanga website.

INSERT MAP - Lake Turkana indicated by Justin's finger.

Jonah seems hesitant but finally nods his consent.

120D   **EXT. CAMP. DAY**   120D

Some of the villagers are being forced by raiders to carry
away the food sacks. Captured goats and children are being
herded away with them.

Overhead: the BUFFALO, taking off.

120E   **EXT. LAKE TURKANA. DAY**   120E

WE SEE the lake and the volcano, desert around it; a brown,
arid, empty, desolate wasteland.

The Buffalo, now overhead, turns and commences its landing
approach.

121   **INT. BUFFALO. DAY**   121

Justin is in the cockpit, immediately behind Jonah and his co-
pilot. He is addressing an envelope.

                    JUSTIN
          Can you land here?

                    JONAH
          I can land, but you don't want to
          go down there. Nothing there but
          crocodiles. Let me take you back to
          Loki.

                    JUSTIN
          I won't be alone for long.

                    JONAH
          Your decision.

                    JUSTIN
          There is something you can do for
          me, Jonah, if you wouldn't mind.

Justin hands him a thick envelope, sealed and addressed but
not stamped.

                    JUSTIN (CONT'D)
          Would you post this for me?

                    JONAH
              (glancing at the address)
          Ah, Rome. So-called cradle of
          civilization.
              (chuckles)
          Down there where you're going,
          people were making tools a million
          years ago.
              (smiles, holds up the
               letter)
          But they didn't have airmail.

He lowers the landing gear, trims for final approach.

122   **EXT. LAKESIDE DESERT. LATE AFTERNOON**   122

A MONTAGE of shots of Justin making his way on foot through
the arid landscape on the margins of the lake.

123   ***EXT. LAKESIDE. PRE-DUSK***   123

The lake is magical in this light: its colours muted pastels
in perfect harmony one with another, its music the call of
water fowl. Impossible to believe - in such country, in such
a light - that any soul on earth might harbour malice.

DISCOVER JUSTIN sitting on a rock, eyes closed, the pistol
resting beside him.

As his eyes open...

DISCOVER TESSA next to him. He reaches out to her. It's as
though Justin knows he has come home. He draws her close. She
rests her head upon his shoulder.

                    JUSTIN
          Now I know all your secrets. Now I
          understand you.
               (pause)
          And now you'll want me to go home.
               (a smile)
          I am home.
               (pause)
          They cheapened your death, made it
          a tabloid scandal. They can't do
          that twice. Yes, I know what they
          did to Arnold...
               (places hand on gun)
          They won't get that chance with me.

124   ***INT. ITALIAN CHURCH, LONDON. DAY***   124

This is not a funeral but a joint memorial service. The
attendance: British-based relatives, friends and colleagues.
For the most part, faces we don't recognize.

PANNING THE CONGREGATION, CAMERA DISCOVERS

HAM AND GUIDO and, two rows behind them, PORTER AND VERONICA
COLERIDGE.

REVEAL PELLEGRIN at the lectern.

                    PELLEGRIN
          Not two years ago and not a mile
          from here Justin Quayle delivered a
          lecture. It was an exceedingly dull
          lecture, for I and not he had
          written it...
               (pauses for a slight
               murmur of amusement)
                    (MORE)

(CONTINUED)

                         PELLEGRIN (CONT'D)
              ...but I'm told the questioning
              that followed was livelier,
              Justin's interrogator being dear
              irrepressible Tessa, whom he
              subsequently took to wife.
                   (pause)
              If we have lost in Justin and Tessa
              two valued friends, the diplomatic
              community has lost a true gentleman
              - courteous, self-effacing, large
              of heart. That he chose to take his
              life in the same remote spot where
              Tessa met her tragic death is a sad
              reflection of his tormented state
              of mind, but also typical of his
              discretion. He would not have had
              us troubled; he would not have had
              us inconvenienced. "Nothing in his
              life became him like the leaving
              it."

Pellegrin steps down from the podium. Returning to his seat,
he passes HAM, on his way to the lectern carrying a Bible.
Pellegrin nods to him. Ham doesn't nod back.

Ham takes his place at the lectern. Opens the Bible.

                         HAM
              I have chosen a text I know Justin
              and Tessa would approve. It's an
              epistle. Non-canonical.
                   (pause)
              "Dear Sandy, Your naïvety is beyond
              belief...."

PELLEGRIN'S REACTION

ANGLE ON HAM'S BIBLE - inside it, THE HANDWRITTEN LETTER
given by Lorbeer to Justin.

                         HAM (CONT'D)
                   (still reading)
              "...Knowing our arrangements with
              KDH and ThreeBees, you send me this
              half-baked report by some bleeding-
              heart diplomatic wife and her black
              lover, and ask me to take action...

ON PELLEGRIN - his future as readable on his face as an
almanac. Damage-limitation measures will be taken in
Whitehall. There will be scandal, blame, recrimination,
enquiries, articles, documentaries, questions in the House.
But ultimately Pellegrin alone will carry the can, and he
knows it.

                                                    (CONTINUED)

                HAM (CONT'D)
      "The only action required, apart
      from shredding the thing, is to
      keep a tighter rein on your
      resident harlot. I want to know
      what she does, where she goes, whom
      she meets...

PELLEGRIN, getting to his feet...

COLERIDGE - enjoying Pellegrin's discomfiture.

                HAM (CONT'D)
      "The issue here is deniability. If
      nobody told us Dypraxa was causing
      deaths, we can't be held
      responsible. But my dear Sandy,
      should it ever become known that we
      closed our eyes to the deaths, none
      of us would survive the scandal.

ANGLE ON JOURNALISTS following Pellegrin towards the door,
mobile phones being pulled from pockets...

                HAM (CONT'D)
      "I still have great hopes of you.
      My love to Gloria. Yours sincerely,
      Bernard."

Ham closes the Bible.

                HAM (CONT'D)
      The author of that letter has told
      you Justin took his own life...

125   ***EXT. LAKESIDE. DUSK***   125

Now even Tessa has gone, leaving Justin quite alone. He has
waited a long time here, seated in perfect stillness on his
rock as the shadows have lengthened around him and the lake's
margins have softened; water, land and sky merging
indistinguishably.

Now we sense that he is no longer alone.

WIDER ANGLE

Around Justin the shadows are moving: formless at first, but
slowly resolving into HUMAN FIGURES, men advancing on
Justin's solitary position, encircling him; men with weapons
in their hands....

There are half a dozen of them: AFRICAN YOUTHS hired for
shillings, these wielding pangas, rifles, knives;

(CONTINUED)

125   CONTINUED: 125

but also the two white killers seen at Kolowa: the SQUAT MAN
WITH THE SHAVEN HEAD and the FAIR-HAIRED MAN. These two are
armed with pistols.

Justin slowly rises from the rock....

OVERHEAD ANGLE - JUSTIN ENCIRCLED

He turns to look behind him, then back again to face those in
front. At last the enemy has a face.

He picks up the 9mm automatic....

...and fires a single round, though not an aimed round. For
this is not self defence, it's provocation, designed for no
other purpose than to ensure himself a clean death.

His attackers respond with a murderous fusillade...

126   *INT. ITALIAN CHURCH, LONDON. DAY*   126

                         HAM
              Bizarre sort of suicide. His body
              bore no fewer than eight bullet
              wounds, from three separate guns -
              none of which was the one found in
              his hand...

ON PELLEGRIN as he exits, pursued by journalists.

                         HAM (CONT'D)
              So who has got away with murder?
              Not, of course, the British
              Government. They merely covered up -
              as one does - the offensive
              corpses....

127   *EXT. NAIROBI RIVERSIDE AREA. NIGHT*   127

HEADLIGHTS from an open lorry and a car are trained on the
marshy burial area as AFRICANS wearing protective face masks
exhume the Dypraxa corpses. Shades of Belsen.

Watching, supervising all of this, is CRICK.

His presence tells us the exhumation is not official. The
bodies are merely being transferred under cover of darkness
to another secret location for re-interment.

                         HAM'S VOICE (V.O.)
              ...though not literally. That was
              done by person or persons unknown.
              So who has committed murder...?

128   **EXT. AFRICAN VILLAGE. DAY**   128

Another mobile clinic in another dusty, unpaved African
village street; AFRICAN medics, wearing the logo of
"ZIMBAMED", doling out Dypraxa to a line of emaciated TB
sufferers - mostly WOMEN and CHILDREN.

            HAM'S VOICE (V.O.)
       ...Not the House of ThreeBees, for
       that no longer exists... nor the
       highly respectable firm of KDH
       Pharmaceutical, which has enjoyed
       record profits this quarter...

As each child receives its medication, a NURSE dips into a
bucket and issues instant rewards: sweeties and cheap Chinese
toys.

            HAM'S VOICE (V.O.) (CONT'D)
       ...and has now licensed ZimbaMed of
       Harare to continue testing Dypraxa
       in Africa....

129   **EXT. NEW KIBERA CLINIC. DAY**   129

Among the shanties, a new permanent clinic has been
constructed and is just beginning to function. A WORKMAN is
still mixing pink plaster in a wheelbarrow, while a NURSE
organizes a line of PATIENTS waiting for treatment.

In the line we recognise JOMO.

On the wall is a veiled plaque.

A car arrives. Out of it steps the tall, dignified figure of
GRACE MAKANGA (40+). To the applause of those watching and
the FLASHES of PHOTOGRAPHERS brought here for the purpose,
she unveils a brass plaque identifying the building as:

"THE TESSA QUAYLE CLINIC - KIBERA"

Tessa's legacy.

            HAM'S VOICE (V.O.)
       ...No, there are no murders in
       Africa. Only regrettable deaths and
       the monuments we erect to them...

130   **EXT. LANGATA CEMETERY. DAY**   130

Ghita laying flowers on the graves of Tessa and Justin...

131   **INT. NEW KIBERA CLINIC. DAY**   131

Inside, the walls are still being plastered. Having finished one wall, the PLASTERER has begun applying his gypsum skim to the remaining three.

ANGLE ON THE FINISHED WALL

It's entirely covered with names; scratched, like frescoes, into the fresh pink plaster.

A YOUNG AFRICAN GIRL finishes scratching the name of her dead mother with a trowel. She hands the trowel to KIOKO.

> HAM'S VOICE (V.O.)
> ...and from those deaths we derive
> the benefits of civilization: oil
> and gas, minerals and medicines –
> benefits we can afford so easily
> because those lives were bought so
> cheaply.

Kioko scratches a name into the wet plaster: "WANZA KILULU"

Roll of the Dypraxa dead.

TRACK WITH CAMERA from the wall to the back door and out through it into

132   **EXT. CLINIC YARD. DAY**   132

A tiny patch of ground has been cleared behind the building. An OLD AFRICAN MAN, using a broken shovel as a trowel, is digging a hole in the raw earth. His small GRANDSON, kneeling beside him, hands him a tuber which he places in the hole, patting earth around it.

Planting a garden.

FADE TO BLACK

PRODUCTION NOTES

The Constant Gardener

A Love Story and a Dedication

Brought to the screen by a convergence of tremendous filmmaking talent from all over the globe, *The Constant Gardener* combines—as only motion pictures can—adventure, social relevance, and emotion.

Director Fernando Meirelles states, "The chance to take on some of the pharmaceutical industry was only one of three elements that made me want to direct *The Constant Gardener*. Another was the chance—the choice—to shoot in Kenya. And it is also and fundamentally a very original love story; a man who marries a younger woman, and it's after she dies that he truly falls in love with her and goes looking for her. It's a beautiful tale, with a touch of the existential to it."

"For me, theirs is a 'retrospective love affair,'" concurs Ralph Fiennes, who plays the title role. "There are two equal parts to this movie. On the one hand, it's a political thriller about corporate wrongdoing, malfeasance and manipulation. On the other, it's about the relationship between Justin and Tessa Quayle. Justin's journey traces not only what Tessa was investigating; he's also playing detective about their relationship. This man rediscovers and re-assesses his own relationship with his wife. It's a wonderful part, because he goes from being a reticent nice guy to being someone who is forced to confront some pretty tough truths about the world. I hope that the audience sees him as a kind of Everyman."

Rachel Weisz, who secured the pivotal role of slain activist Tessa Abbott Quayle, adds, "The love story and the political thriller element are completely interlocked—one doesn't happen without the other, and that's the cleverness of both John le Carré's novel and Jeffrey Caine's adaptation. Because of

Justin's love for Tessa, he goes on a journey of discovery where he reaches a new level of self-knowledge, but he also discovers a huge political scandal."

"At first glance, Justin appears very passive," says Meirelles. "He's a civilized British gentleman, a polite diplomat who lives by a code. He doesn't fully know what Tessa does; sometimes he would like to interfere, but he doesn't, not because he's weak but because he has an agreement with her, and he lives by that code as well. We were all interested in exploring just why Tessa was interested in Justin. She needs an anchor and Justin keeps her sane; he's so controlled, and she's so passionate."

"Justin is a passionate—gardener," notes Fiennes. "There's an internal quietude about gardeners, this sensitivity to watching something live and grow, and caring about how something will flourish and bloom. To me, that was all key to Justin. Why does he marry someone as opinionated and passionate as Tessa? I think they're drawn to one another because opposites do attract."

Screenwriter Jeffrey Caine remarks, "Ralph and Rachel made me believe totally in the passion and the tenderness of the Tessa-Justin relationship."

The character of Tessa Quayle is drawn from real life. John le Carré dedicated *The Constant Gardener* to a passionate activist and tireless charity worker named Yvette Pierpaoli. As part of an on-screen dedication in the film's closing credits, he describes her as having "lived and died giving a damn."

In 1999, at the age of sixty, Yvette Pierpaoli was killed, along with two other aid workers and their driver, in a car crash in Albania. At the time, Yvette was a representative for Refugees International, part of her lifelong commitment to help other people. That vocation had been set from the age of 19, when she left her native France for Phnom Penh. It was there that le Carré chanced to meet her, during the mid-1970s. From their first encounter, Yvette used every means at her disposal, whether feminine wile or bullish argument, to win the author over, as he remembers:

> But it was all for a cause. And the cause, you quickly learned, was an absolutely non-negotiable, visceral requirement in her to get food and money to the starving, medicines to the sick, shelter for the homeless, papers for the stateless and, just generally, in the most secular, muscular, businesslike, down-to-earth way you can imagine, perform miracles...
>
> And though by age, occupation, nationality and birth my Tessa was far removed from Yvette, Tessa's commitment to the

poor of Africa, particularly its women, her contempt for protocol and her unswerving, often maddening determination to
have her way stemmed quite consciously so far as I was concerned, from Yvette's example.

— *"The Constant Muse,"* The Observer, *February 25, 2001*

"THE WORLD'S BIGGEST DRAMA"

"The world's biggest drama is not found in Europe or the
Middle East or North America—the world's biggest challenges
and dramas are found in Africa."

—*[quote from United Nations emergency relief coordinator Jan
Egeland] Warren Hoge, "U.N. Relief Director Appeals for Help in
Crises Throughout Africa,"* The New York Times, *May 11, 2005*

When independent British film producer Simon Channing Williams read
an advance copy of John le Carré's *The Constant Gardener* in late 2000,
he wrote an impassioned letter to the author's lawyer, Michael Rudell. In
the letter, the producer pleaded his case for being given the chance to turn
the novel into a film. When Rudell replied and suggested a meeting, Channing
Williams volunteered to fly from London to New York that same evening.
The producer explains, "I wanted to prove to him how serious I was about
making it into a movie, because I thought the book was so extraordinary. It
delves into the rapaciousness of big business, the abuse of the African peo-
ples, governmental corruption, and at the root of it all, an utterly compelling
love story. It was such a heartfelt, angry book, and, sadly, I believe it will remain
relevant for many, many years to come."

As the movie took shape, screenwriter and novelist Jeffrey Caine took
on what he calls the "professional challenge" of adapting the novelist's
work. Caine comments, "I'm a long-time admirer of John le Carré's writing and have always felt—in common with many of his readers—that the
films made from his novels have rarely done them justice. *The Constant Gardener*
struck me as having the potential to be a strong film; an emotional personal
love story wedded to a timely political theme and a suspenseful structure.
For me, the heart of the tale was always the human story of Justin and
Tessa; that of a politically uncommitted man discovering only after her
death the true nature of the woman he loved and thereafter devoting him-

self to continuing her work, growing even closer to her than he was during her lifetime."

Caine adds, "It was important to Simon and to le Carré that he approve the screenwriter, so the final step before I was hired was a lunch at which I had to convince le Carré that he'd come to the right store. Seems I managed that.

"During the development process—which took over two years—he sent in quite a few sets of notes on the various drafts and attended some of the script meetings. Happily, he's movie-wise as well as book-wise; he knows that in order to make a novel work on the screen, much has to be done differently. In fact, he often urged me to change even more than I was inclined to change."

He retained the book's nonlinear approach, noting, "Because of what happens to Tessa—killed off on page one—it was necessary to use flashbacks. Otherwise we wouldn't be able to engage emotionally with Tessa and Justin. The balancing act for me was to provide a sufficiently intriguing forward thrust to the narrative without giving away too much of the plot too soon and without sacrificing either the personal story of Justin's growth to understanding or the underlying thematic content."

The 2002 film (released in many territories in 2003) *City of God* alerted Channing Williams to an exciting new director, Fernando Meirelles, who had successfully visualized, and conveyed, a powerful story from a part of the world most people never get to see.

BIG PHARMA

John le Carré's novel addressed the issue of corporate social responsibility and giga-profits in one of the world's biggest business sectors, the pharmaceutical industry. In a syndicated article at the time of the novel's publication [2001], the author wrote:

> I might have gone for the scandal of spiked tobacco...I might have gone for the oil companies...but the multinational pharmaceutical world, once I entered it, got me by the throat and wouldn't let go. Big Pharma, as it is known, offered everything: the hopes and dreams we have of it; its vast, partly realised potential for good; and its pitch-dark underside, sustained by huge wealth, pathological secrecy, corruption and greed.

As *City of God* continued to run in theatres (and, in the U.S., for over a year), director Fernando Meirelles cleared his schedule to seriously research *The Constant Gardener*. He says, "I'm from Brazil, and over the past several years, we have been making generics, and if you try to make cheap versions of patented medicines, you very quickly learn a lot about the unbelievable power of the drug industry lobby. I've been reading about this for the past few years—on Oxfam's website, for example—and I realized that making a film is a good opportunity to prod them. *The Constant Gardener* is not so much political but, as a person from a developing country, I understand what happens in one. So I felt I could represent the Kenyans' interests in the movie."

The behavior and business practices of some pharmaceutical manufacturers have come under increasing scrutiny in recent years, with wider coverage in the media and stronger pressure from numerous consumer watchdogs and interest groups. Le Carré's novel contributed to a greater awareness among the general public of the industry's potential to do harm as well as good.

In order to justify their pricing and close guarding of patents, some drug companies repeatedly cite the high costs of the research and development (R&D) and clinical trials they must undertake to bring a new product to the market. Watchdogs counter that drug companies rarely incur these R&D costs themselves, but instead avail themselves of publicly funded research—and then guard the results. Many have voiced doubts about the $800 million figure that the industry claims is needed to bring a new drug to market, pointing to the disparity between the pharmaceutical manufacturers' R&D and their marketing budgets. The latter, the argument goes, is where the big money is truly allocated.

> In the past two years, we have started to see, for the first time, the beginnings of public resistance to rapacious pricing and other dubious practices of the pharmaceutical industry. It is mainly because of this resistance that drug companies are now blanketing us with public relations messages. And the magic words, repeated over and over like an incantation, are research, innovation...But while the rhetoric is stirring, it has very little to do with reality. First, research and development (R&D) is a relatively small part of the budgets of the big drug companies—dwarfed by their vast expenditures on marketing and administration, and smaller even than profits. In fact, year after

year, for over two decades, this industry has been far and away the most profitable in the United States. (In 2003, for the first time, the industry lost its first-place position, coming in third, behind "mining, crude oil production," and "commercial banks.") The prices drug companies charge have little relationship to the costs of making the drugs and could be cut dramatically without coming anywhere close to threatening R&D.
—*Marcia Angell, "The Truth About Drug Companies,"* New York Review of Books, *July 15, 2004*

Activists also accuse some Big Pharma companies of ignoring innovation to develop barely distinguishable "me-too" drugs based on proven "blockbusters," focusing their efforts on what ails the rich Western market—e.g., heart disease, baldness and geriatric impotence—while slighting and outright ignoring the unprofitable, rampant diseases of the developing world. The latter countries are being ravaged by AIDS, tuberculosis, and malaria (the last-named affecting approximately 500 million people a year and, by some estimates, killing a child approximately every 20 seconds). While these nascent nations bear an outsize burden of disease, they account for only a tiny fraction of Big Pharma's profits.

When all other arguments fail, some spokespeople for the pharmaceutical industry remind us that theirs is not a philanthropic enterprise, and that their greatest responsibility is to their shareholders. This, at least, is a point on which the companies and their critics agree; the industry has made hundreds of billions of dollars (in 2002, total sales reached an estimated $430 billion).

Beginning in 1997, Brazil has been able to successfully reduce its death toll from AIDS by half, defying the pharmaceutical manufacturers and ignoring the threat of trade sanctions to provide low-cost anti-retroviral drugs. The country also fielded an aggressive prevention campaign. Despite the progressive model Brazil has instituted, the efforts in Meirelles's native country have not been replicated worldwide.

Seconding Meirelles in his passion for the material, Simon Channing Williams remarks, "I'm not a political animal. But what we are exploring is happening today, in the world we all live in."

Meirelles studied Brian Woods's and Michael Simkin's U.K. [Channel 4] program *Dying for Drugs* as documentary evidence on the practices of some pharmaceutical companies in the developing world. Jeffrey Caine states, "Most of the research had already been done by le Carré and is in the book. What isn't in the book was provided by some very well-informed medical contacts and fed to me in small spoonfuls as directed. It's all very well to say, as no doubt some will, 'Big Pharma is too obvious a target.' But evils need to be publicized and to go on being publicized as long as they exist, which is forever."

Ralph Fiennes states, "There are huge questions about Big Pharma. Fernando gave me some background material, including *Dying for Drugs*. The companies are not obliged to disclose a lot of information about how they test or make their drugs. There's big, big money involved in the development, patenting, and marketing of a new drug; there's no question that the pharmaceutical industry has one of the most powerful lobbies in the United States. I'm sure there are companies out there wanting to produce good, effective drugs at reasonable prices but a lot of people want—and need—to ask tough questions of the industry as a whole."

Rachel Weisz agrees with Fiennes. She notes, "It's David and Goliath; the little people taking on the great big corporations. I believe that pharmaceuticals are second only to oil now; it is a massive business. They make all this money, yet people in developing countries can't afford the drugs that could save their lives."

Dr. Bonnie Dunbar, a molecular biologist and former professor at Houston's Baylor College of Medicine who now makes her home in a suburb of Nairobi, vouches for accuracies in the film's plot. She comments, "I was quite fascinated by the parallels with things I have experienced in my professional life. The lobbying by the international organizations, as well as the amount of money poured into cover-ups ring true to me. Hopefully the murder aspect of the story is not true-to-life, but when there's big money involved..."

Caine says, "I don't expect *The Constant Gardener* to change the conduct of international pharmaceutical companies. It might—best case—draw the attention of audiences to certain widespread practices of Big Pharma and in some small way help create a climate for more responsible behavior. The most important thing for me is that the film should illustrate the nature of commitment."

THE EARLY LOCATIONS

After final casting and preparations in the winter and spring of 2004, production began in May.

The production headed to Berlin to shoot scenes involving the watchdog group Hippo Pharma, which becomes a crucial part of Justin Quayle's quest to uncover the truth behind his wife's death. Locations in Berlin included the Lehrter Stadtbanhof, for Justin Quayle's arrival by train in Germany; offices in the Academie der Kunste, standing in for British High Commission offices; the Residenz Hotel, where Justin experiences first-hand the brutal methods that the Dypraxa drug manufacturers will resort to in order to avoid exposure; and the venerable Studio Babelsberg.

After two weeks in Germany, the production moved to London for several days of work. A space at the Tate Modern Gallery (located on the South Bank of the River Thames) was used as the lecture hall where Justin first meets Tessa, while St. Mary Magdalene Church in Paddington became the scene of a memorial service.

Other London locations included the Liberal Club, standing in for the gentleman's club where Sir Bernard Pellegrin has an illuminating lunch with Justin. The scene includes Jeffrey Caine in "a nifty little cameo as a club porter. I'd been banging on to Fernando about the actors improvising on my lines, and Fernando had been spreading his hands and saying, 'Actors have to have some space to do this; what can I do?' Then he directs me in a role written with only one line of dialogue and finds me adding lines as I go. He said, 'Now you know what I have to put up with.'"

DEEPER INTO AFRICA

Saving the most significant phase for last and affording Fernando Meirelles the visual and storytelling opportunities he had counted on, the production moved to Kenya in early June for nearly two months of shooting in Nairobi and other parts of the country. This had come about through diplomacy from Simon Channing Williams with government officials. Le Carré's novel had delineated a deeply corrupt government in Kenya, which led to the book's originally being banned there.

Even so, that had not prevented Kenyans from bringing in multiple copies from abroad—and circulating them among friends and neighbors. Nor did the novel's criticism of the British diplomatic corps prevent the current, real-life High Commissioner, Edward Clay, from offering his support to the filmmakers.

"One of our very early visits was to Edward and his deputy Ray Kyles," says Simon Channing Williams. "As much as anything else, it was the encouragement and support of the British High Commission that allowed us to convince our backers, insurers, and completion guarantors that Kenya was a viable place for us to film."

Meirelles adds, "Edward helped us in many ways. Our actors were able to meet people from the High Commission, and went to their houses to see how they live. We had a lunch in London with diplomats working in Kenya. Our feeling, talking to them and being in their offices, was that the High Commission these days is like any other business. It looks like Unilever or Shell; it's really about doing business, and making opportunities for business. Although it's been forty-two years since British rule in Kenya ended, there's still a tie that binds—now mostly for different reasons."

Referring to both the original novel and the screen adaptation, Edward Clay states, "In the first place, it is a work of art. You don't have to accept that British diplomats are really like this, you don't have to accept that particular pharmaceutical companies in Kenya are the ones the author had in mind. It is a fine love story, wrapped up in a parable that has real power and credibility. But the problems that le Carré describes are potential as well as actual. Kenya is not the only country where he could have set the story, but it was a good setting. It could have been another government; it could have been another industry. But the point about the risks and the temptations of exploitation between the rich and powerful and the poor and vulnerable is very important and very telling."

Danny Huston, cast as the British High Commission's Head of Chancery, Sandy Woodrow, comments, "Modern diplomacy is all about business, and about trying to encourage commercial ventures. I also had a meeting in London with two gentlemen who shall remain nameless, since they worked for [British Secret Service agencies] MI5 and MI6. The more time I spent with them, the more I felt that they actually were like the people portrayed in the book. They have an extraordinary, sometimes spectacular way of not answering a question you ask them."

Edward Clay and his staff briefed actors and filmmakers on the political, economic, and social context of Kenya—both as it was when John le Carré wrote his novel, and as it is now, just a few years later. He says, "Africa is not an undifferentiated basket case; there are successes, and some of the countries that used to be on their backs are now doing quite well. Kenya has done relatively badly by comparison over the last twenty years, fundamentally because of problems of governance. I suppose I wanted to make the point that when le Carré was writing his book, he was writing about a Kenya of a particular era which was a very plausible setting for the story that he wanted to tell. And that now that the film is being made, we're in a Kenya where government and society have decided and voted quite decisively for a change—that Kenya will not be a byword for poor governance and corruption as it used to be."

Channing Williams reports, "The final link in the chain allowing us to film in Kenya was the government and at every juncture, our Kenyan production partners Blue Sky Films and I were met with great courtesy and understanding. There was a real willingness and commitment to enable us to film there."

Given the subject matter, the Kenyan government proved to be remarkably accommodating to the filmmakers. The Hon. Raphael Tuju, Minister of Information & Communications, states, "*The Constant Gardener* is very critical of Kenya, and it was unprecedented that this ministry would support it and license it. But I went ahead and made sure that we did so, because if we didn't support it being filmed here it was still going to be filmed somewhere else, and it would still be critical of Kenya in the past, with respect to issues like corruption."

Meirelles felt that his perspective was different from the outset. He muses, "John le Carré wrote a story about a developing country and big business from the point of view of a person from the First World. When I read the book, I put myself in the other position. I saw myself in Africa, with the big companies coming in. In some respects, Jeffrey Caine's script tells the story through Kenyan eyes and, as a person from the Third World, I identified more with the Kenyans than with the British."

Caine notes, "The Kenyan setting attracted Fernando to the film, I think. But what he inherited was a story told through British eyes, embedded in a British post-imperial subculture with which he wasn't wholly familiar. Unsurprising, then, that he would want these elements de-emphasized and the African elements given more prominence, without tipping the story out of balance. This I think we achieved."

Channing Williams welcomed the new light that Meirelles cast on the film's subject matter. He notes, "I feared we might get stuck in a 'middle-class British male' box. When Fernando signed on, suddenly all those middle-class prejudices were thrown out the window. Instead, we were getting an entirely new vision of the world that le Carré wrote about, visualized from a deeply intelligent foreign national's point of view. Fernando's perception is all to do with character as opposed to class. Our British class structure is not important to him; it was great that we could get away from that, and tell the story as seen by 95 percent of the rest of the world."

Production designer Mark Tildesley comments, "When I first read the book, I thought it was something that described and would appeal to my father's generation. But then we went to these clubs in Nairobi and it's like a time warp, even at the British High Commission. They try to get funky and tell you they ride a bike to work, but then they ring a bell for breakfast and people come in to serve it with white gloves…What we really needed to do was to make people have a sense of Africa, and care about Africa in order to understand the story. So it couldn't all be cricket and gin-and-tonics."

Ralph Fiennes recalls, "Fernando was very keen to incorporate African footage, the colors and the faces. When I was first told that he was going to direct, what I hoped was that he would make Africa a keystone for the film, and that's just what he did."

Meirelles' "Third World perspective" also ensured that, in addition to the hundreds of extras employed on the shoot, a large proportion of the cast would be African (the film features Kenyan nationals in nearly three dozen speaking roles). Moreover, the British crew was joined by more than seventy Kenyan crew members represented across all departments, in addition to drivers, caterers, location hire staff, and laborers.

Channing Williams states, "All of these people, on both sides of the camera, were there by right; those jobs and roles should have been theirs, and were. There is an amazing well of talent in Kenya and I hope that, in some small way, our presence there might help to alert others to what is on offer."

Although Meirelles regards Kenya as "almost the third principal character in the movie," the filmmakers originally considered shooting most of the Kenyan scenes in South Africa, where there is a thriving film industry and a more established infrastructure. Channing Williams notes, "The idea was for us to come to Kenya to see where the book was set and then go down to South Africa. But I'm delighted to say that, within 24 hours of our arrival, Fernando and I both knew that we didn't want to move from Kenya at all. Of course, there were serious problems in terms of insurance, in terms of the perception that Kenya was a very dangerous place to be— which we found not to be the case. We fought long and hard; it was very clear from the outset that Kenya was where we should be."

Mario Zvan, executive producer for the film's Kenyan production partners Blue Sky Films, reveals, "East Africa is very different from South Africa, and Fernando and Simon understood that immediately. The people look different, the vegetation is different, the light is different, the buildings are different. Shooting this story in South Africa would have been like filming a Boston tale in Miami."

"We were very concerned that this looked real," adds Meirelles' friend and collaborator of many years, director of photography César Charlone. "We were trying to show the truth, to be as faithful as we could be, using real locations and natural light. If a mortuary was lit with fluorescents, we went with fluorescent lighting. It was very important to us not to choose locations because they were more filmic or more beautiful.

"Then, as we started getting deeper into the project, it was as if we were dealing with two different realities, two different worlds. There was Justin's old world, where he came from, with the British High Commission. As he finds out more about Tessa, she becomes his door into a new world, the real Africa that he had been unable or unwilling to see. We determined that Justin's world (England) would in cool greens, while Tessa's world (Africa) would be in warm reds."

"Fernando and César were determined to present as authentic a view as possible, to try to make something remarkable," comments Bill Nighy, who plays Bernard Pellegrin. "I'd worked in Morocco but I'd never been to Kenya or anywhere else in Africa. The sights, sounds, and smells are like nowhere else. It's more than just a backdrop because *The Constant Gardener* is an African story, dealing with how the West uses the continent as a laboratory."

"One of the great things about the experience was that we shot in real places in Nairobi," says Ralph Fiennes. "Fernando was very keen to use real people in the background. There isn't a strong film infrastructure in Kenya, so we weren't shooting with professional, practiced extras. The feeling towards the film on the part of the people was very positive; they engaged with something that was happening in their neighborhood. Simon and Blue Sky did an amazing job to make sure that we were not seen, as films coming in are usually seen—a lot of people shouting into walkie-talkies and crashing through a community, ignoring the sensibilities of the people who actually live there. I never felt any resentment or negativity. The sensitivities of the locals were not only acknowledged, they were embraced by the camera so that they felt part of the project."

Kenyan extras casting co-ordinator Emily Mbonga clarifies, "It's not that we don't have an infrastructure for filming in Kenya; it's more that it had been forgotten." Mbonga found the majority of the white extras through open casting calls among local amateur theater groups. Other extras were recruited from the professions being portrayed; for example, the members of the press intruding on Tessa Quayle's funeral are all journalists and photographers working in Kenya.

"The key to creating a character is mostly imagination and when you are in the actual place, it is there for you on a plate," says Fiennes. "On a subtle level, you're already responding physically and emotionally to the environment."

Rachel Weisz adds, "Nothing against South Africa, but the Kenyan landscape has a particular spirit and you can't just try to mimic that somewhere else. I can't separate Kenya from the story, or the story from Kenya. What's also important is that we have helped the existing infrastructure, so that more films might shoot there in the future."

Pete Postlethwaite, who appears as Dypraxa's elusive creator, Lorbeer, says, "You do your work, you read the book, you figure where your character is at. But actually going to Kenya puts it all into focus, like a magnifying glass that you could use to burn your hand."

ON LOCATION IN KENYA

The first scenes to be filmed in Nairobi were at the suburban Lord Errol Restaurant, used as the venue for the British High Commission cocktail party that crystallizes Tessa Quayle's and Dr. Arnold Bluhm's drive to expose the hypocrisy and greed of those in power. The Lord Errol is named for the notorious womanizing aristocrat, whose story was the subject of another film shot in Kenya, 1988's *White Mischief*.

The unit next filmed at the private Royal Nairobi Club and, at the other end of the spectrum, a city dump near River Road in Nairobi's "combat zone." The dump is home to a community of down-and-outs, most of them solvent abusers. Glue-sniffing is a big problem among street-dwellers in Nairobi, both adults and small children alike; extending beyond even the sadly recognizable addictive elements, glue fumes are said to stave off hunger.

For the scenes of Tessa Quayle's hospitalization and discovery of the deadly effects of Dypraxa, the production shot at Pumwani, a working maternity hospital catering to Nairobi's poorest residents—and the center of a scandal at the time of filming. The local press was full of reports concerning high incidents of mistaken infant identity at the hospital; other reports pointed to the hospital's higher-than-average mortality rate. While acknowledging that they are fighting a losing battle, Pumwani's Matron Bridget Mbatha, who appears as a hospital administrator in the film, defended the institution against these charges. She argues that undernourished, unhealthy mothers and their underweight newborns are inevitably less likely to survive, particularly when they are rushed to an understaffed, ill-equipped hospital as an emergency measure when a birth assisted by untrained, backstreet clinic operators has gone awry. Following one day's filming at Pumwani, Danny Huston sorrowfully remarked that it was "a truly heartbreaking place."

Additional locations in and around Nairobi included the Nairobi City Mortuary (where the scene of Tessa's body being identified was filmed), Langata Cemetery, the Kenyatta Hospital records office, Boskie's aircraft hangar at Wilson Airport, and a golf course at the Karen racecourse. Sandy Woodrow's house in the film is in reality the suburban Nairobi home of the European Commissioner.

Another private house in a Nairobi suburb was used as Justin and Tessa's home. It belongs to the mother of *The Constant Gardener*'s wardrobe supervisor, Elizabeth Glaysher, who grew up there. Her mother Sonia, had once before worked on a film shot in Kenya; she was Ava Gardner's body double in John Ford's *Mogambo* (1953). Sonia's gardener, Celia Hardy, was the "gardening coach" for Ralph Fiennes. With the exception of some flowering plants added for color and texture by the production design crew, Justin's on-screen garden is the result of Celia's year-round handiwork.

The weekday vegetable market in the village of Kiambu was used as the location for the Three Bees Mobile Clinic, where Justin finds Kioko, brother of Dypraxa casualty Wanza Kilulu. Kioko is played by 16-year-old student Donald Opiyo, who was picked up from his boarding school and driven to the set on each shooting day. Although the mothers and babies lining up to receive "free testing and treatment" at the Three Bees Clinic were hired extras, the hundreds of customers and vendors in the scene are the real people of Kiambu, going about their daily business.

At the end of the shooting day in the Kiambu market, Fernando Meirelles noticed that a crowd of school children had gathered behind a barricade blocking off the set. He approached them and called out, "Okay, who wants to be in a movie?"

All hands went up, but only a dozen children were selected to run up the road, as César Charlone captured the scene from the bed of a pickup truck. Knowing that there was some disappointment among the other children, Meirelles returned to the horde of kids and shouted, "Okay, everybody!" The barricade was lifted, and a stampede of school kids engulfed the crew. The amount of dust raised precluded this latter shot from appearing in the finished film; it was one of the few spontaneous moments that couldn't stay in. In addition to shooting whenever the spirit moved them and wherever they could, Charlone would occasionally hand a lightweight camera to Ralph Fiennes to shoot, for example, Justin's POV of a plant in a nursery or of his household staff offering their condolences after Tessa's murder. Simon Channing Williams dubbed the method "the 'if it moves, shoot it!' philosophy. You know, the focus-pullers had one of the hardest tasks on this film and, incredibly, nine times out of ten, they would get it perfectly."

"With Fernando, nothing is rigidly choreographed," notes actor Donald Sumpter, who plays the secretive Tim Donohue. "You get people buzzing around, and actually going in and out of focus. You get real impressions of things, which is fantastic."

"Fernando and César have a very low level of bureaucracy around them," adds Rachel Weisz. "Things happened very fast on set! César would just move the camera and hang a light bulb. It was as if we were a small documentary crew filming on location, and it allowed for things to be very organic and spontaneous; it felt like reportage, or guerrilla filmmaking."

"It was a delightful way to work," says Danny Huston, who speaks from past experience as a film director himself. "Film stock is so sensitive these days that you don't have to use so many lights, and you don't have to hit your mark every time. This wasn't a Hollywood film where you needed your back-light, a key light, and a little click in your eyes to make sure you looked absolutely glamorous. The story our film tells needed reality."

The Kiambu Police Chief's office was used for the police station sequence where Justin is taken in for questioning. Detective Inspector Deasey, who arrives at the scene, is portrayed by Ben Parker, a real-life press officer at the U.N. in Nairobi.

Kiambu also hosted the scene of the improvised toll that Justin pays to some enterprising street kids. The toll-takers were played by reformed street kids who now reside in a rehabilitation center outside Nairobi. The kids' lunchtime talk centered on the equitable distribution of the fee they'd received from the production for their day's work; at last report, they seemed to have settled on new shoes and socks for all of the boys at the center, and possibly a soccer ball and a television set. The boys' chaperone happened to be Jo Cottrell Boyce, the teenaged son of well-known British screenwriter Frank Cottrell Boyce, who had taken a year off from his studies to do volunteer work in Kenya.

"HOW ARE YOU?" IN KIBERA

The film's opening scene was filmed in Nairobi at the largest slum in sub-Saharan Africa. Kibera is a sprawling shantytown of approximately 600 acres with an estimated population of 800,000 people (some say 1.2 million), most of whom live in makeshift huts constructed of scrap lumber, mud, and corrugated iron—and lacking sanitation, running water, and electricity. The word *kibera* means "forest" in the language of the Nubian mercenaries who originally settled the area after being demobilized from the armies of British East Africa. Gradually, more and more itinerant laborers made Kibera their home, many of them with the intention of saving enough money from working in the capital to move back to their native villages.

Today, there are very few trees in Kibera, and every Kenyan tribe is represented among its residents. The "streets" are a labyrinth of raised pathways and shallow trenches winding among streams of raw sewage. The main drag is a working railway line that bisects the shantytown. Residents set up shop along the tracks, laying out anything of conceivable value to anyone.

Fernando Meirelles says, "It's hard to believe, but I think that Kibera is actually worse than the *favelas* of Rio where we filmed *City of God* and the TV series, *City of Men*. César Charlone and I had spent a lot of time in the *favelas*, and Kibera was still a shock for us. I can't even imagine what the British crew members thought. The poverty was…sobering." As it turned out, many of the Kenyan crew members had never even been to Kibera, and were equally taken aback.

Poverty in Kenya averages 56 percent, which means that 15 million people live on $.80 a day; Kibera residents live on even less than that. Hundreds of people walk along the road to the slum at the beginning and end of every workday they are going to and from work so as not to pay $.30 for bus fare.

As schoolmaster David Mogambi Nyakambi pointed out, "People want to live in Kibera because it is close to where the work is, and it is relatively safe; people rarely steal here because there is nothing to steal." Mogambi, whose schoolyard served as the unit base for the Kibera shoot and whose belief in the bright future of Kibera's children inspired all who met him, was killed in automobile accident in June 2005.

Although some people do manage to save enough money to move back to their native villages farther up country, many more are born and die in Kibera. In addition to the absence of even the most basic amenities, the residents are severely afflicted by the AIDS epidemic; it is estimated that one in six Kenyans is HIV-positive, and the percentage is surely higher in Kibera. As in all of sub-Saharan Africa, the number of orphans in Kibera rises daily; the social services needed to look after them are all but nonexistent.

Without fail, flocks of tiny children gleefully greet every foreigner who visits Kibera, shaking hands and addressing them (particularly, a *mzungu* [white outsider]) with, "How are you? How are you? How are you?"

Jeffrey Caine reports, "[That phrase is] their only English. What impressed me was how friendly and happy the kids were. They follow you everywhere, not begging for hand-outs but putting out their hands to be held."

The city-within-a-city welcomed the production for over a week. Confirming what schoolmaster Nyakambi said, reports suggesting that Kibera would be hostile and dangerous were not found to be the case by the cast and crew of *The Constant Gardener*. Their experience was unforgettable—and, for many, exhilarating.

A unit base was set up in the schoolyard of the Raila Odinga Educational Centre, which is named after the Member of Parliament for the Langata area that includes Kibera; he is also the Minister for Roads and Transport.

Bernard Otieno Oduor, a radio presenter and singer who was cast as Jomo in *The Constant Gardener* following an open audition, reports, "The former regime was pretty uncomfortable with the novel because it implicates the government in one way or another. The film tells the truth about what happens in developing countries, what no one wants to talk about because of the big profits. It's amazing that the current government supported the film; Raila Odinga was on the set, having lunch with the producers and chatting, knowing exactly what the film is about."

Some 2,000 Kibera residents worked as extras, and others worked as guides and porters for the film crew, negotiating difficult terrain and also stepping in as security guards and interpreters.

Even so, muses Fernando Meirelles, "All was calm. One day, I just went out with César Charlone, a camera assistant, Simon Channing Williams, and Rachel Weisz and Hubert Koundé—and we shot Rachel, as Tessa, interacting with locals."

Several cast members who were not on-screen in the opening sequence nonetheless made a point of visiting the Kibera set to watch Nick Reding's SAFE Theatre troupe stage a play about AIDS, as movie cameras recorded the performance. Actor/director Reding, who appears in the film as Crick, originally came to Kenya from Hollywood to help build a clinic in Mombassa. While there, he recognized the need to impart information about HIV/AIDS by engaging entire communities, and hit upon the idea of street theatre as a means of getting the message across in a uniquely effective way. His SAFE (Sponsored Arts for Education) group has since performed along truck routes from Mombassa to Nairobi.

Meirelles saw a short film made by the SAFE group, and asked Reding to turn it into a play for inclusion in the movie. The play scenes were filmed live before hundreds of Kibera residents, with Rachel Weisz and Hubert Koundé, in-character as Tessa Quayle and Dr. Arnold Bluhm, also in the audience.

Reding comments, "A lot of people are very reluctant even to say the word 'AIDS.' If you can do a big enough show and really entertain them, if you can even make them laugh, then you can get them to talk about it. Wherever we've done the show, it starts a huge debate, with people discussing the use of condoms and so on. AIDS in Africa is a disaster on an unimaginable scale; drugs are becoming more available now, and the people need to understand how and why to take them."

This educational approach to the crisis is crucial. Rumors spread quickly in a tight-knit community such as Kibera, and the stigma of AIDS can lead people to neither avail themselves of treatment nor make the efforts to prevent the virus from spreading. An indigenous organization, AMREF (African Medical Research Foundation), now has the capacity to distribute anti-retroviral drugs free of charge to all HIV-positive Kibera residents through a neighborhood clinic. A spokeswoman admits that the greatest challenges are encouraging people to get tested for AIDS in the first place and, if they prove to have the virus, to sign up for treatment. Like the film's character of Jomo, however, a large proportion of Kibera residents are unwilling to be tested—and unprepared to accept an HIV-positive diagnosis.

The production was determined from the outset to give something back to Kibera. In addition to providing jobs for as many locals as could be accommodated each day on the set, the construction crew created a play area and soccer playing area, reinforced the roof of a dilapidated church, and built a bridge across a wide sewer to enable emergency vehicles to access residents living at the bottom of a ravine.

"We built the bridge, and later put a 10,000-liter fresh water tank next door to it. Our tank will provide water for free to everybody," informs Simon Channing Williams. "We also built a ramp up to the railway line, in a similar position to one we used for the camera as a substitute for a crane shot, which will particularly help the elderly and the handicapped." Previously, the incline to the railway track was so steep that only agile children could scale it with ease.

"We talked to the community leaders first," says locations manager John Chavanga. "They then talked to the people and explained our purpose for being there, and how it could benefit the community. We employed about 2,000 people in various areas and built some lasting structures. It was quite an experience for the locals. This was the biggest film ever to shoot in Kibera, and I think they learned a lot from the process. There is a lot of talent there—Bernard Otieno Oduor, who plays Jomo, was brought up in Kibera. They have drama schools and theatre groups. Who knows? Maybe one of the local kids will grow up to become a big actor like Ralph Fiennes."

"Kibera was so much bigger than anything I could possibly imagine," says Rachel Weisz. "The kids are just incredible. They have none of the 'stranger danger' Western kids are encouraged to feel. The spirit of the place is somehow so much stronger than the poverty. After three days, I started to catch that and relax into it, because of my character; I think that was where Tessa felt truly comfortable."

"Kibera makes you understand Tessa," agrees Caine. "You go home feeling you want to help [the kids], improve the material quality of their lives, and this the production company has done."

LAKES AND LOIYANGALANI

After more than a month, the unit left the Norfolk Hotel and the cool, diesel-choked mountain air of downtown Nairobi. The production headed south, by road, to the village of Ol Tapese, near Lake Magadi in the Rift Valley. A few colourfully painted wooden shacks appear to constitute the whole of Ol Tapese, yet the seemingly barren landscape is in fact teeming with magnificent life. Red-clad Masai herdsmen seemingly materialize from the vast expanse. Emily Mbonga says, "In Kenya, we always joke that you can be driving along a road and there's nobody; then you have an accident and a million people show up. It may look remote, but there are always people out there." Extras casting co-ordinator Lenny Juma had previously visited the area around Ol Tapese to hire a crowd of Masai to appear in a scene; more came throughout the day, to sell handicrafts to the crew, get a drink of water, or just to observe the filming.

The unit moved nearby to an archaeological site on the spectacular cliffs of the Rift Valley to shoot a car chase in which Justin, in a borrowed Fiat, is pursued by the initially unseen driver of a Land Rover. Simon Channing Williams reveals, "Literally two miles down the road from where we were shooting, I'd gone to check the location we were planning to use for our helicopter shots—only to find that the Smithsonian Institute had taken our spot; they had found remains of our forebears that were 900,000 years old, the oldest human remains found on earth."

Having spent the night in a tented camp, the unit arrived at remote Lake Magadi (standing in for the more northern Lake Turkana in a climactic scene), which resembles the surface of the moon.

The comparison is still a valid one, as the 104-kilometer alkaline lake is encompassed by vast salt flats that crunch underfoot like frozen snow. Flamingos and insects seem to be the only form of life on or near the lake, which exhibits an otherworldly roseate coloring. But, a Masai can and will appear out of nowhere through the blinding heat, either on foot or on a bicycle, while savaged flamingo carcasses at the edge of the lake indicate the presence of predators in the vicinity.

During a break from shooting at Lake Magadi, Rachel Weisz agreed to appear in a television spot for the U.N.'s World Food Program, which camera operator Diego Quemada-Diez in turn volunteered to film for the charity. "The WFP, particularly Regional Information Officer Laura Melo, was an invaluable source of information and help for the production," states Channing Williams. The WFP spot will show the actress walking across the endless, empty expanse at the edge of Lake Magadi, trailed by a group of local school kids, the children of workers at the Magadi Soda Company (which owns this area of the Rift Valley). Magadi Soda provides for its workers' housing, schools, and healthcare. The contrast with Kibera was not lost on cast and crew.

The cast and crew returned briefly to Nairobi before travelling north to the village of Loiyangalani, on the southeastern shore of the real Lake Turkana (the world's largest desert lake), where they would shoot the Southern Sudan-set scenes of Camp Seven.

Loiyangalani is a two-and-one-half day drive, or a two-hour plane trip, from the capital. Some of the crew members arrived in the Buffalo aircraft that would be used in the sequence itself, although others were fortunate enough to travel in twelve-seater aircraft that afforded spectacular views of the volcanoes around Lake Turkana. Although breathtakingly beautiful and supporting fish and birdlife, the lake itself is so extremely alkaline that its water is virtually undrinkable. The world's largest population of crocodiles inhabit the lake.

"Loiyangalani is basically a remote piece of real estate consisting of lava floes," says Blue Sky Films' Mario Zvan. "There's not much else, really; a few doum palm trees around bits of lake where there is fresh water. It's very dry, very hot, and very inhospitable, about as far as one can get from civilization as we know it. The book actually sets a scene in Loiyangalani, but we went there instead to film a part set in Southern Sudan. We couldn't shoot those scenes in the Sudan both because of the political situation and the lack of infrastructure."

Even so, remembers Channing Williams, "When I first went to Loiyangalani, I had no idea what we were actually looking at. You can't begin to imagine somewhere like it, nor can you overestimate the difficulty of filming in such a place."

"Logistically, it was very tough," agrees locations co-ordinator Robin Hollister. "It's at the end of a non-existent road, so all of your supplies have to be flown in from 600 kilometers away."

The shores of Loiyangalani are home to a hardy few, among them several different tribes. These include the Turkana, the Samburu (cousins of the Masai), the Rendille, and the El Molo (the smallest African tribe).

"When we realized that we would be right in the middle of their village, we felt that the community would have to benefit from our being there," explains Hollister. "We requested that they set up a committee to represent all the vested interests of the community, of all the different tribes, so that we could deal with one entity rather than several thousand people. Here was a once-in-a-decade opportunity for them to get a little bit of commerce into their economy."

The "once-in-a-decade opportunity" that Hollister cites is an understatement; it was more than a decade earlier that he had been in Loiyangalani for location shooting of Bob Rafelson's *Mountains of the Moon* (which was released in 1990). He notes how the local tribespeople still refer to births as having taken place during the period when that film was shooting, and speculates that children born in 2005 will be told that they were conceived during "the time of the second movie."

"I believe that all of the groundwork we did with the film committee in Loiyangalani was absolutely vital," says Channing Williams. "It was all about building trust. We could have got permission from the local council to shoot there and just gone in and done it, but I believe that would have been dreadful and ultimately damaging. With Robin's help, I made sure that we established a relationship with Senior Chief Christopher, the local police inspector, and the entire community."

Some crew members were primarily housed in tents resembling a military encampment, on the edge of the existing airstrip, even as a neighboring airstrip was lengthened by the production to allow for the landing of a massive Buffalo aircraft. Two lodges (one of them The Oasis, which is featured in John le Carré's novel) were also taken over by the unit to house cast and crew, with much-appreciated swimming pools; temperatures ran high at the location, and there was no shelter from the sun, nor much from the dust and the wind off the lake.

As in Kibera, a welcoming community and the constant companionship of dozens of friendly, fearless children made for an unforgettable work experience for those who were there. Between takes, Ralph Fiennes and two of the other actors were frequently obliged to ask for their setside chairs to be vacated by local children, only to have the kids settle into their laps and perch on the arms of their chairs.

At dawn, local extras and laborers gathered on the set to sing and dance in celebration of the day's work. The community was encouraged to take advantage of the unit's drinking water supply, and the resulting lines saw flamboyantly dressed Samburu warriors lined up waiting patiently with camera technicians, while Turkana girls sporting Mohawks and/or henna applications stood with unit drivers, and naked toddlers wove in and out. Locals were also advised that they could visit the doctor and nurses in the unit's first aid tent. Word of the medical attention traveled quickly, as an elderly Turkana walked from his home forty kilometers away to consult the doctor about his joint pains; the diagnosis was the all-too-familiar combination of old age, malnutrition, and dehydration.

For the Sudanese border raid sequences, a few days passed before the winds abated and the South African special effects crew was able to safely set fire to the specially-built prop huts without risk to the real surrounding palm-frond huts that are home to many Turkana families. A professional livestock theft-prevention unit was brought in to portray the raiding party. Veteran stunt co-ordinator Rory Jansen pronounced these riders and their horses to be among the best he had ever worked with; this was also high praise given the heat, the extremely dangerous terrain, and the hundreds of untrained men, women, and children employed as extras for the chaotic sequence. One of the riders, given a camera, was able to shoot footage—while on horseback, at breakneck speed. In the midst of the orchestrated mayhem, a Buffalo plane repeatedly flew over at dizzyingly low levels yet perfectly on cue; its pilots were accustomed to performing these feats of daring for real, having made perilous food drops across the border in Sudan.

The final day of the Loiyangalani shoot also marked Simon Channing Williams' investiture as a tribal elder. That evening, the village square was transformed into an open-air cinema by Filmaid (a charity providing entertainment and diversion to refugees around the world). During a ceremony filled with dancing and speeches from local dignitaries, Channing Williams was presented with the feathered headdress and the pair of carved walking sticks that symbolize his new status. The producer had become so familiar with the territory since his first (advance) visit six months earlier that he was already regularly making the eight-kilometer trip to take urgently need food and water supplies to the remote El Molo tribe.

Among the many other initiatives undertaken by the new tribal elder and co-producer Tracey Seaward were providing mattresses and linens for the children who board at the local school, and giving the production facilities fee to the entire community—in the form of a trust fund for local children to receive a secondary education. The duo also arranged for any and all disposable props, costumes, and construction materials to be distributed by the mission to Loiyangalani's neediest.

The last days of July saw the final leg of the shoot, as Ralph Fiennes and a reduced unit filmed in Lokichoggio. That town has been, since 1989, the hub of the international relief effort in Southern Sudan. Scenes of Justin Quayle's arrival in Lokichoggio were filmed, along with aerial views of the Kenya-Sudan border and a food drop from a Hercules aircraft.

"Africa will live within me because of a couple of very different memories," says Fernando Meirelles. "There is the amazing landscape and the people who warmly received us. It's such a beautiful place. But I can never, and will never, forget the problems the continent has, which were so much bigger than I was expecting. We talked about this on location; when a British man says that a country is poor, that's one thing, but when a Brazilian man like myself says it, well, that's something else. And what of their future? When I think that one in six Kenyans is HIV-positive and it's not just HIV, it's hepatitis, it's tuberculosis, and all kinds of illness all over Africa…it's frightening. It's hard to have hope for the future, and yet we must."

THE FUTURE

Recent developments show cause for both hope and concern:

> The Food and Drug Administration has approved the first generic triple-therapy AIDS cocktail, opening the way for

American taxpayer dollars to be used to buy cheaper medicines for use in poor countries. Assuming the drugs made by the approved company…are priced at a third to a half of brand-name ones, charities and poor nations getting Bush administration money will be able to treat two or three times as many patients. The goal of the United States is to underwrite the treatment of two million patients internationally by 2008, said Randall L. Tobias, who administered the $15 billion President Bush promised two years ago for the fight against AIDS. The United States donates up to a third of the budget of the Global Fund to Fight AIDS, Tuberculosis and Malaria, which can be spent on any drug approved by the World Health Organization. Most of the rest of the money from Mr. Tobias's office goes to the President's Emergency Plan for AIDS Relief, which serves 13 African countries, Haiti, Guyana, and Vietnam, and can be used only for F.D.A.-approved drugs…The F.D.A. approval, which came this week, is for marketing only outside the United States—in effect, only in poor countries, since the drugs are patented in Europe, Japan, and other rich markets…

—*Donald G. McNeil Jr., "A Path to Cheaper AIDS Drugs for Poor Nations,"* The New York Times, *January 26, 2005*

The number of AIDS patients receiving life-saving drug treatment in poor or middle-income nations rose 60 percent in the past six months, the World Health Organization said Wednesday, largely because of a huge influx of international aid funds and a growing determination by governments to confront the pandemic…Still, anti-retroviral treatment reaches only one in eight needy people in the developing world, leaving an estimated 5.1 million people without such protection. Last year, the disease took more than three million lives, three-fourths of them in sub-Saharan Africa…One in every six people who die of AIDS is under 15—more than half a million deaths a year, the [World Health Organization] report said…The United States spent $2.4 billion fighting AIDS last year, mainly in Africa, and Congress has approved $2.9 billion for the current fiscal year.

—*Sharon LaFraniere, "Poor Lands Treating Far More AIDS Patients,"* The New York Times, *January 27, 2005*

Kenya's Health Ministry admitted that it had failed to distribute $54 million meant to fight HIV/AIDS, malaria and tuberculosis, a day after a U.S. Ambassador said the delay amounted to "a death sentence." Health Ministry spokesman Richard Abura blamed the delay on conditions set by the World Bank and the International Monetary Fund. The conditions included contracting an agency to ensure the money was well spent and hiring 78 accountants to manage the funds. He said the government has struggled for more than nine months to meet the donor conditions and had approved the hiring of the accountants Wednesday...
—*Smita P. Nordwall, "Kenya fails to distribute aid funds,"* USA Today, *February 3, 2005*

Billions more dollars will be needed to curb the spread of AIDS in Africa, but as countries increase their donations, the amounts will be less important than how well they are spent and in what context, a new report from the United Nations AIDS program said yesterday...An estimated 25.4 million people in Africa are infected now...The report is available online at www.unaids.org.
—*Lawrence K. Altman, "A U.N. Report Takes a Hard Look at Fighting AIDS in Africa,"* The New York Times, *March 5, 2005*

Kenya has never seemed to be able to live up to the potential of its rich farmland and staggeringly beautiful valleys...Some 56 percent of the population lives below the poverty level...But far from the noise, pollution and public and private crooks of Nairobi, the village of Sauri, practically smack on the equator, is an example of a better way to do things. It is one of two test cases for the United Nations' ambitious program to cut poverty in half by 2015...The United Nations plan, spearheaded by the economist Jeffrey Sachs, seeks to expand the program to the entire district, and then all over Africa. But that will happen only if rich countries make good on their promise to ratchet up foreign aid to 0.7 percent of G.D.P. by 2015. Britain, France

and Germany have all put out timetables for meeting the goal.
The United States, the world' s richest country, has yet to do
so.

—*Editorial,* The New York Times, *May 5, 2005*

The production's initiative to return something to the communities that
welcomed the film shoot continues unabated. Simon Channing Williams
has set up a charitable trust, saying, "This is not about supporting a charity
that has a large overhead and new 4x4 vehicles. Rather, our intention is to
directly support the areas that have helped us so much, as well as a few spe-
cific others. We are right now concentrating on Kibera, Loiyangalani, and the
El Molo; also, on orphans of AIDS and the street children of Nairobi.
Additionally, we are researching programs that care for children on a non-
denominational basis; water programs for the areas in which we have
filmed; and the performing arts. Why that, you may ask.

"The answer is, so many people have told us how important film can be
in terms of increasing understanding at every level; Nick Reding has
already proven how theater can make a difference, with his SAFE group. So
now, the movies must do their part."

CAST AND CREW CREDITS

FOCUS FEATURES Presents in association with the U.K. FILM COUNCIL
a POTBOILER Production in association with SCION FILMS

RALPH FIENNES   RACHEL WEISZ

THE CONSTANT GARDENER

DANNY HUSTON   BILL NIGHY   PETE POSTLETHWAITE

Casting Director
LEO DAVIS

Makeup & Hair Designer
CHRISTINE BLUNDELL

Music Composer
ALBERTO IGLESIAS

Costume Designer
ODILE DICKS MIREAUX

Editor
CLAIRE SIMPSON

Production Designer
MARK TILDESLEY

Director of Photography
CESAR CHARLONE

Co-Producer
TRACEY SEAWARD

Co-Producers
HENNING MOLFENTER
THIERRY POTOK

Executive Producers
GAIL EGAN
ROBERT JONES
DONALD RANVAUD
JEFF ABBERLEY
JULIA BLACKMAN

Based on the novel by
JOHN LE CARRÉ

Directed by
FERNANDO MEIRELLES

Screenplay by
JEFFREY CAINE

Produced by
SIMON CHANNING
WILLIAMS

THE CAST, IN ORDER OF APPEARANCE

Justin Quayle	Ralph Fiennes	1ˢᵗ Journalist	Steenie Njoroge

Justin Quayle . . . . Ralph Fiennes
Tessa Quayle . . . . Rachel Weisz
Arnold Bluhm. . . . . . . Hubert Kounde
Sandy Woodrow . . . . . . Danny Huston
Miriam . . . . Daniele Harford
Officer in Morgue . . . . . Packson Ngugi
Jomo's Wife. . . . . Damaris Itenyo Agweyu
Jomo. . . . . Bernard Otieno Oduor
Sir Bernard Pellegrin . . . . . . Bill Nighy
Porter Coleridge. . . . . . . Keith Pearson
Dr. Joshua Ngaba . . . . John Sibi-Okumu
Tim Donohue . . . . . . Donald Sumpter
Ghita Pearson . . . . Archie Panjabi
Crick. . . . . Nick Reding
Sir Kenneth Curtiss . . . Gerard McSorley
Gloria Woodrow . . . . Juliet Aubrey
Wanza Kilulu . . . . . Jacqueline Maribe
Kioko . . . . Donald Apiyo
Lorbeer . . . . Pete Postlethwaite
Mustafa . . . . Samuel Otage
Birgit . . . . Anneke Kim Sarnau
Grace Makanga. . . . . . . Mumbi Kaigwa
Athletic Unshaven Man . . . . John Moller
Shaven-Headed Man . . . . Andre Leenheer
Kenyan Newsreader . . . . Lydia M. Manyasi

1ˢᵗ Journalist . . . . Steenie Njoroge
2ⁿᵈ Journalist . . . . Stuart Wheeler
Mike Mildren . . . . Chris Payne
Esmerelda . . . . Nyajima Jial
Hospital Administrator . . Brigid M. Kakenyi
Nurse. . . . . Katherine Damaris
Doctor . . . . Christopher Okinda
Police Driver. . . . . Ainea Ojiambo
Policeman 1 . . . . Peter King Nzioki
Policeman 2 . . . . . . Kirumburu Ng'ang'a
Det. Inspector Deasey . . . . . Ben Parker
Immigration Official. . . . . . John Keogh
Club Servant . . . . Jeffrey Caine
Arthur Hammond . . . . . Richard McCabe
Guido Hammond . . . . . Rupert Simonian
Birgit's Secretary. . . . . . . Teresa Harder
Uniformed Policeman . . Thomas Chemnitz
Karl . . . . Joe Christopher Rhode
        Edgar Nicolas Rhode
Crossing Guard . . . . Eva Plackner
Maude Donohue. . . . . . Claire Simpson
Jonah Andika. . . . . Sidede Onyulo
Aid Worker. . . . . . Chris Lightburn-Jones
Ana. . . . . Ann Achan
Sudanese Man. . . . . . Dang Wuor Diew
Harry Woodrow . . . . Ben Gardiner

The Crew and the Credits

Directed by . . . . Fernando Meirelles
Produced by . . . Simon Channing Williams
Screenplay by . . . . Jeffrey Caine
Based upon the novel by John le Carré
Executive Producers . . . . Gail Egan
Robert Jones
Donald Ranvaud
Jeff Abberley
Julia Blackman
Co-Producer. . . . . Tracey Seaward
Co-Producers . . . . . . Henning Molfenter
Thierry Potok
Director of Photography . . César Charlone
Production Designer . . . . . Mark Tildesley
Editor . . . . Claire Simpson
Costume Designer. . . Odile Dicks-Mireaux
Music Composer. . . . . . Alberto Iglesias
Makeup & Hair Designer. Christine Blundell
Casting Director. . . . . Leo Davis
1st Assistant Director . . . . . Richard Styles
2nd Assistant Director . . . . . Carlos Fidel
3rd Assistant Director . . . . Susan Drennan
Script Executive. . . . . . . Sarah Golding
Script Supervisor . . . . . Susanna Lenton
Script Consultants . . . . Christiane Riera
Bráulio Mantovani
Production Sound Mixer. . . . .
Stuart Wilson, A.M.P.S.
Boom Operator. . . . . Orin Beaton
Supervising Art Director. . . . . Chris Lowe
Art Director . . . . Denis Schnegg
Set Decorator . . . . Michelle Day
Supervising Prop Master . . . .
Chris Lightburn-Jones
Location Prop Master. . . . . Arwel Evans
Graphic Designer. . . . . . . Carol Kupisz
Assistant Art Director . . . . . Coralie Lew
Assistant Prop Buyer . . . . . Kathryn Pyle
B Camera Operators . . . . . Alastair Rae
Diego Quemada-Diez
Focus Puller . . . . Olly Tellett
Clapper Loader . . . . Peter Byrne
Stills Photographer. . . . . Jaap Buitendijk
Key Grip. . . . . Paul Hatchman
Production Manager . . . . . . Lisa Parker
Production Co-ordinator . . Kate Penlington
Assistant Production Co-ordinator. . . . . .
Scott Jacobson
Assistant to Simon Channing Williams . . .
Claire Broughton
Assistant to Gail Egan. . . . . Abbie Browne
Assistant to Ralph Fiennes . . . Kelly Messias

Assistant to Rachel Weisz . . Natalie Borlaug
Assistant to Fernando Meirelles for 02 Filmes
Eduardo Lyon
Assistant Casting Director . . . . Lissy Holm
Supervising Production Accountant. Will Tyler
Location Accountant . . . . . . Jon Miller
Assistant Accountants . . . . . Justin Miller
Andrew MacLean
Gaffer. . . . . Andy Long
Rigging Gaffer . . . . Billy Tracey
Assistant Costume Designer . . . Jane Petrie
Standby Costumes . . . . . . Kate Chilcott
John Denison
Caroline McCall
Makeup and Hair Artist. . . . Lesa Warrener
First Assistant Editor . . . . . . Keith Mason
Post-Production Supervisor. Alistair Hopkins
Post-Production Co-ordinator . . Bek Leigh
Supervising Sound Editor . Joakim Sundström
Sound FX Editor . . . . Nick Adams
Additional FX Editor . . . . . Jennie Evans
ADR Editor . . . . Paul Wrightson
Music Editor . . . . Tony Lewis
Foley Artist. . . . . Nicolas Becker
Foley Editor . . . . Sam Southwick
Foley Mixer . . . Anthony Faust, A.M.P.S.
Assistant Sound Editor . . . Richard Kondal
FT2 Trainee . . . . Ravi Desai
Dialogue Coaches . . . . Sandra Butterworth
Clifford De Spenser
Sandra Frieze

Kenyan Unit

Executive Producers for Blue Sky Films . . .
Mario Zvan
Jim Shamoon
Production Supervisor . . . . . Nick Laws
Production Manager . . . . . . Hemal Shah
Supervising Location and Unit Manager. . .
Robin Hollister
Casting . . . . Emily Mabonga
Crowd Casting . . . . Lenny Juma
Casting Assistant . . . . Mwakalafu Muniafu
Production Co-ordinator . . Alison Ngibuini
Turkana Co-ordinator. . . . . Harriet Stanes
Production Assistants. . . . Consolata Karani
Muthoni Ngacha
Phylis Andika
Shiv Mandavia
Angela Kombu
Location Managers. . . . . Bernard Gathogo
John Chavanga
Location Assistants . . . . . . Ali Mwangola
Faiz Hassan Salim

Location Co-ordinator . . . Kevina Navisino
Unit Manager . . . . Chris Wilding
Location Plumber . . . . Gabriel Gitau
Location Electrician . . . . Stanley Njuguna
Unit Assistants . . . . Johnson Karuki
David Kareihti
Wycliff Obote
Elias Mwiti Kimari
Patrick Musyimi
Omari Shaban
Joel Karo
John Baraza
Musa Ali Kamau
Samuel N. Munene
Stephen Mukora
Titus Malinda
B Camera Focus Puller . . . . . Telfer Barnes
B Camera Clapper Loader . . Chris Summers
C Camera Clapper Loader . . . . John Evans
Justin Quayle POV Camera . Ralph Fiennes
1st Assistant Director . . . . . Konga Mbandu
2nd Assistant Director . . . . . Wambui Kairo
3rd Assistant Director . . . . . Nick Njache
Toll Boy's Director . . . . . Jo Cottrell Boyce
Production Runners . . . . Peter Mudamba
Faith Wambui Njoroge
Godwin Muhati
Serah Mwaniki
Estia Mophat Osore
Charles Bukeko
James Sangoro
Arthur Muiruri
Lupita Nyongo
Art Director . . . . Vittoria Sogno
Prop Master . . . . Nick Thomas
Art Buyer . . . . Julia Seth-Smith
Art Dept. Assistant . . . . Teresia Mwangi
Props Assistant . . . . Michael Silva
Storeman . . . . Sam Kombo
Assistant Storeman . . . . Beatrice Tabitha
Prop Man . . . . Peter Ndungu
Prop Assistants . . . . . . Simon Waithaka
Richard Warui Maingi
Elizabeth Nyagah
Gilbert Michira Rondani
Key Assistant Accountants . . Evelyn Atsiaya
Herman Mbugua
Assistant Accountants . . . . Emmanuel S.
Wakhungu
Margaret Muthoni
Haron Komoni
Key Grip . . . . Steve Obunde
Grips . . . . Paul Atoni
Peter Kioko

VTR Assistants . . . . Peter Murimi
Amar Desai
Camera Trainee . . . . John Mungai
2nd Boom Operator . . . . . . Mark Kihara
Best Boy . . . . Benson Maingi
Generator Driver . . . . . George Mbugua
Electricians . . . . Francis Ouma
Saul Ogada
Ezekiel Andika
George K. Kahura
Peter Njogu Kamau
Construction Manager . . . . Graham Cole
Construction Assistant . . . . . . John Silva
Head Carpenter . . . . Evans Gitau
Carpenters . . . . Henry Oginga
Patrick Kabaru
Paul Njonjo
John Chege Gachoka
Peter Ndungu
Mungai Solomon N. Kamau
Stephen Gitau
Frederick Kago
Moses Mugera
Kuria Joseph Githau
Hazron Mwangi
Julius Gatheri
John Juma Juma
James Wachira
John Mwangi Maina
Stanley Chege Kariuki
John Njoroge Kimani
Standby Carpenter . . . . . Samson Maitemi
Welders . . . . John Sulwe
Samuel Ndungu
Head Painter . . . . Paul Mungai Kinyanjui
Painters . . . . Sylvester Otieno
John Ogutu Radol
Lawrence Wambu
James K. Kuria
Standby Painter . . . . . Lawrence Wathiga
Bender . . . . Dancan Nzuka Ivutha
Masons . . . . Peter Mbugua
Francis Ngugi
SPFX Supervisor . . . . . Cordell McQueen
SPFX Foreman . . . . Mickey Kirsten
SPFX Assistants . . . . Colin Athanasius Silva
Randy Selwano
Patrick Obero
Kevin Adcock
Tyrell Kemlo
Wireman . . . . Jason Leinster
Stunt Co-ordinator . . . . . . Roly Jansen
Assistant Stunt Co-ordinators . Charles Kembero
Mo Marais

169

Stunt Crew . . . . Daryl Andrews
Jake Mervin
Stunt Driver . . . . . . David Sandenbergh
Wardrobe Supervisor . . . Elizabeth Glaysher
Wardrobe Assistants . . . . . . Chris Kariuki
Rana Mekapi
Joseph Mwangangi
Tessa Neylan
Catherine Muthee
Willie Kyalo
Charles Muli Mutiso
Ann Kombo
Cyprine Atieno
Domie Mueni
Anne Kalui
Anne Wairimu Kariuki
Sari Fitter . . . . Urrashi Patel
Makeup Artist . . . . Gillianne Obasu
Makeup Assistant . . . . . . Hannayi Barbara
Makeup Trainee . . . . Zara Pasha
Set Medic . . . . Lawrence Mugambi
Africa Air Rescue Paramedics . Stephen Nyaga
Victory Omufila
Location Nurses . . Mercy Muthoni Waweru
Emily Mulaya
Jerioth Njoki
Catering . . . . Rolf Schmidt,
Horseman's Catering
Armourer . . . . Ben Pont
Assistant Armourers . . . Ulius M Ambuche
Johnson N Mwanyika
Ernest M. Muchiri
Jeremiah Makori
Rufus K. Kutto
Samuel Ewoi
Romano Okoro
Antistock Theft Unit Inspector . . . .
Asher Muthamia
Veterinary Surgeon . . . . . . G. G. Ngumi
Rider/Vet . . . . Peter Omondi
Rider/Ferrier . . . . Bojein Magongo
Rider/Saddler . . . . Bernard Kingoo
Riders . . . . Moses Odhiambo
Neville Mokua
Eric Moia
John Kiprop
Michael Anemba
Raymond Ochieng
Kennedy Ndeto
Simon Chesesio
Peter Rukioya
Braham Muteria
Nelson Nakure
Kennedy Mugambi
Cyrus Karema

Peter Nduriri
Pius Kivuti
Mechanic . . . . S Nyangarama
Animal Wrangler . . . . Wachira Muiragania
Fire Safety Officer . . . . . Wilson Wachiuri
Fire Safety . . . . Godfrey Ohutso
Hack Waiganjo
Ibrahim Lela
Erick Macharia
Steven Kyengo
Transport Supervisor . . . . . . Eddie Aniere
Transport Co-ordinator . Rashid Mohammed
Transport Assistant . . . . . Bernard Gatheru
Action Cars/Transport Assistant . Moses Wanjau
Action Cars Mechanic . John Njoroge Wainaina
Drivers . . . . James Wachira Kamahiu
Edward Mugane
George Waiyaki
Stephen Gichoi
Ben Muchiri
Stephen Irungu
James Kariuki
Muli Leonard
Joseph Njoroge
Jacob Ochieng
Ferdinand Yeswa
Willy Ngaruiya
Joshua Wambua
Jarad Angima
Johnson Macharia
Dickson Kariuki
Steven Ogola
Boniface Kariuki
Steven Ndegwa
Mike Kioko
Charles Kyengo
Francis Mulwa
Francis Muhia
Alex Kimani
Joseph Kimani
John Njoroge
Peter Macharia
George Atsiaya
George Keegan
James Macharia
James Mwangi
Joseph Waithaka
Nick Waweru
Patrick Mungai
Peter Githaiga
James Kalaa
Charles Munene
Gideon Gitonga
George Kimani
Rueben Gitau

Loiyangalani Drivers . . . . . . John Kamau	Shipping Company. . . . . . . Filmline Ltd.
James Maina	Kalpesh Solanki
Boro Waro	Tented Camps Supplied by . Ker & Downey
Lawrence Mathea	Safaris Ltd.
Yunis Mangia	Martin Seth-Smith
Samuel Okoth	African Safari
Samson Mathu	Adventures
Ephantus Tauna	Asad Anwar
Daniel Mutugi	Security . . . . Security Group
Roba Yahani	Kenya Ltd.
Ilow Baltor	
John Njoroge	"Huruma"—AIDS Play
Phillip Amba	Directed by Nick Reding
David Muiruri	
Mark Odera	Performed by
John Maina	The Kizingo Arts Troupe
Patrick Mungai	Lucy Achieng, Elzabeth Karanja,
Samuel Rasha	Sele Mzamil, Suleiman Bakari, Juma Musa,
Mohammed Hussan	Jane Obada, Florence Chamba,
James Ngatia	Triza Musimbi, Benson Obiva,
Justin Gathumbi	Ibrahim Chitaya,
Peter Murage	Eric Mutua, Leonard Ongaya, Abdallah Juma,
Simon Kinyua	Anne Mwikali, James Osoo
Jarad Muiruri	Produced by
Saidi Latoya	Sponsored Arts for Education (S.A.F.E.)
George Murage	Reg. U.K. Charity No.1097369
John Waithaka	
Frederick Chepsror	GERMAN UNIT
Hussein Salim	
Noor Mangia	For Studio Babelsberg GMBH
Victor Biwott	Production Manager . . . . Sonja B Zimmer
Joseph Waithaka	Production Co-ordinator . . . Anne Helmer
Sadik Mohammed	Co-Production Co-ordinator . . . .
Banadick Orbora	Katja Hoerstmann
Daniel Mwai	Production Secretary . . . . . Julia Schulze
Joseph Kingangi	Assistant to Simon Channing Williams . . .
Helicopter Supplied by . . . Everett Aviation	Leonora Penglase
Aerial Unit Pilot . . . . Simon Everett	Assistant to Henning Molfenter . . . . . .
Aerial Operator. . . . . . . Harmon Cusack	Mirjam Weber
Buffalo Aircraft Supplied by	Production Runner . . . . Helga Löbel
Sky Relief (Kenya) Ltd.	Accountant . . . . Steffi Hiller
Buffalo Pilot . . . . Andrew Cliff	Assistant Accountant . . . . Tilmann Vierzig
Buffalo Co-Pilot . . . . Blake Few	Unit Manager . . . . Mark Nolting
Buffalo Aircraft Painted by	Location Supervisor . . . . . Markus Bensch
Flying Pictures Ltd.	Location Manager . . . . . Christopher Doll
Air Charters Supplied by. . . . Z. Boskovich	Location Scout . . . . Frank Seeger
Air Charters	Set Manager. . . . . Sven Herrmann
Pilots . . . . Andrew Allen	Assistant Location Manager . . . .
Daniel Barton	Franziska Strutz-Zander
Victor Chege	Set Production Assistants. . . Sarah Bungartz
Gad Kamau	David Miller
Dennis Neylan	Manuel Kreuzpaintner
T.A.D. Watts	Nicola Schreiter
Prosthetics . . . . Animated Extras	Art Director . . . . Christian Schäfer
Matt Smith	Prop Master . . . . Joey Weber

Prop Buyer . . . . Alexandra Pilhatsch
Storeman . . . . Friederike Beckert
Lead Man . . . . Christian Ehlert
Set Dressers . . . . Florian Speidel
Ulrich Passauer
Lisa Loher
Standby Carpenter . . . . . Matthias Prange
Assistant Prop Master . . . . . Oliver Rose
Art Department Runner . . . . Daniel Fabry
Prop Drivers . . . . Moritz Dirks
Matthias Haase
2nd Assistant Director . . . . Thorne Mutert
3rd Assistant Directors . Ulrike Schaare-Kringer
Till Hohenberger
Crowd Assistant Directors . . Susanna Nedza
Sabine Schulmeyer
B Camera Operator . . Franz Xavier Kringer
B Camera Focus Puller . . . Nicole Dierken
C Camera Operator . . . . . Ergun Cankaya
C Camera Focus Puller . . . . Birgit Dierken
C Camera Clapper Loader . . Ole Ziesemann
Dolly Grip . . . . Robert Wedemeyer
Additional Grip . . . . Hannes Tröger
Video Operator . . . . . . Christian Wehrle
Camera Trainee . . . . . . Sebastian Gross
2nd Boom Operator . . . . . Matthias Richter
Rigging Gaffer . . . . Peter Fritscher
Electricians . . . . . . Benjamin Dreythaller
Sven Trebus
Florian Niedermeier
Andre Schwemmin
Thomas Gosta
Martin Koenig
Wardrobe Assistants . . . . . Sparka Lee Hall
Liza Brzonskalla
Wardrobe Trainee . . . . . Carolin Koenig
Makeup Assistant . . . . . Petra Schaumann
Casting Director . . . . . Annette Borgmann
Extras Casting . . . . Iris Müller
Dialogue Coach . . . . Martin Höner
Stunt Co-ordinator . . . . . . Armin Sauer
Transportation Co-ordinator . Jens Enderling
Transportation Secretary . . . Oliver Kueper
Drivers Captain . . . . . . Marian Goepel
Drivers . . . . Silke Werner
Katja Heissig
Axel Huebner
Daniel Huhn
Grit Menzzer
Till Hennig
Frank Gust
Petra 'Peti' Misaila
Dennis Erdmann
Birk Mueller
Marlene Woznicki

Nobert Mentorp
Knuth Sorgers

LONDON UNIT

Production Co-ordinator . . . . Janine Abery
Assistant Co-ordinator . . . Shanna Baynard
Office Runner . Dominic Channing Williams
Location Managers . . . . . . Alex Gladstone
Jonah Coombes
Unit Manager . . . . Grant Hall
Locations Assistant . . . . . . Asha Sharma
Crowd 2nd Assistant Director Candy Marlowe
Production Runners . . . . Scott Davenport
Emily Perowne
Lara David
James Keaton
B Camera Focus Puller . . . . Mark Milsome
B Camera Clapper Loader . . Harry Bowers
Video Operator . . . . . . Chris Thompson
Trainee Camera . . . . Jason Dully
2nd Company Grip . . . . Tony Turner
Camera Car Driver . . . . Johnny Ott
Best Boy . . . . Anthony Burnes
Rigging Gaffer . . . . . . Gary Donoghue
Electricians . . . . Rob Rabson
Paul Molloy
Generator Operator . . . . Jim Wall
Rigging Electricians . . . . . . Bob Walton
Chris Bryant
Warren Ewan
Steve Cussell
Gary McKerr
Rocky Burnes
Draughtsman . . John Stephen Forrest Smith
Art Department Assistant . . . Dale Manning
Prop Master . . . . Brian Lofthouse
Dressing Props . . . . Eddie Baker
Prop Men . . . . Barry Chapman
David Roberts
Mark French
Construction Manager . . . . . Rob Brown
Standby Painter . . . . Tommy Roberts
Standby Carpenter . . . . Cathal MacIlwaine
Standby Rigger . . . . Chris Hawkins
Costume Assistants . . . Charlotte Wiseman
Christy Watson
Colin May
Katy Hackney
Laurie Saint-Hillier
Lou Durkin
Sharon Long
Costume Truck Drivers . . . . David Kipling
Chris Wateman

Makeup and Hair Assistants . Kirsten Chalmers
Nuria Mbomio
Makeup and Hair Trainee . . . Julius Goosen
Transport Co-ordinator. . . . Waseem Barlas
Drivers . . . . Paul Graham
Jimmy Walters
Joe Savino
Ben Harrington
John Burden
Jamie Burden
Martin Colmar
Ian Colmar
Ray Thompson
Tony Driver
George Andrews

FOR U.K. FILM COUNCIL

Production Executive . Brock Norman Brock
Head of Business Affairs . . . . . Will Evans
Head of Production Finance . Vince Holden
Head of Physical Production. Fiona Morham

FOR SCION FILMS

Production Executive . Nicole Carmen-Davis
Head of Legal and Production . Megan Davis
Legal & Business Affairs . . . Ben Thomas
Production Assistant . . . . . . Laura Tatton

FOR MOONLIGHTING FILMMAKERS (PTY) LTD.

Production Executives for Moonlighting . .
Philip Key
Genevieve Hofmeyr
Production Manager . . . . . . Nicci Perrow
Production Co-ordinator . . . . Dylan Voogt

Completion Bond . . . . Film Finances Inc.
Graham Easton
Legal . . . . Richards Butler
Richard Philipps
Vicky King
Insurance . . . . . . AON/Albert G. Ruben
Kevin O'Shea
Banking Services . . . . . Barclays Bank PLC
Camera Equipment Supplied by . Arri Media
Lighting Equipment Supplied by . . . . . .
Arri Lighting Rental
Publicity . . . . McDonald & Rutter
Jonathan Rutter
Liz Miller
Sarah Clarke
Electronic Press Kit . . . . . . Special Treats
Colin Burrows
Philip Ayers
Sean Hill

Clearances . . . . Now Clear This Research
Jay Floyd
Michelle Dunton
Shipping Companies . Dynamic International
Travel Services Supplied by . . . . Showtravel
Luis Rosa
Walkie-Talkies . . Wavend Communications
Health & Safety Advisors . . . .
JHA Film Safety Partnership
Originated on . . . . Kodak
Laboratory . . . . Soho Images
Laboratory Project Supervisor . . Nigel Horn
Laboratory Contacts . . . . . . John Taylor
Tone Davies
Telecine/Rushes . . . . The Machine Room
Technical Director . . . . . Darryl Huxley
Rushes Co-ordinator . . . . . Rachael Steed
Rushes Colourist . . . . . . Lorraine Lydon
Supervising Colourist . . . . Mick Vincent
Re-Recorded at . . . De Lane Lea, London
Re-Recording Mixers . . . .
Michael Prestwood Smith
Sven Taits
Re-Recordists . . . . Steve Hancock
Philip Mark Freudenfeld
Robert Killick
Foley Recorded at . . . . Atlantic Post
Title Design by . . . . Fig Productions
Richard Morrison
Ally Mee
Facilities . . . . One Post Production
Paul Sullivan
Digital Intermediate . . . . Framestore CFC
Colourists . . Asa Shoul and Adam Glasman
Producer . . . . Maria Stroka
Senior Producer . . . . Claire McGrane
Executive Producer . . . . . . Jan Hogevold
Digital Assembly . . . . . Steve Wagendorp
Scanning and Recording Manager . . . . .
Andy Burrow
Scanning, Recording and Digital Cleanup . .
James Clarke
Dan Perry
Annabel Wright
Jonathan Dredge
Film Mastering Engineer . . . Alistair Hamer
Title Compositing . . . . . Luke Drummond
Computer Graphics . . . Tomorrow London
Creative Agency
Post-Production Script . . . . . Sapex Scripts
Digital Visual Effects by . . Framestore CFC
Digital Supervisor . . . . . . Adrian De Wet
VFX Executive Producer . . . . Drew Jones
VFX Producers . . . . Charles Howell
Michael Davis

Compositors. . . . . Corrina Wilson
                         Adrian Metzelaar
VFX Editor . . . . Roz Lowrie
VFX Avid Editor . . . . . . Tom Partridge
Data Operations . . . . Cal Sawyer
Editing Equipment . . . . Hyperactive
                         Broadcast Ltd.
Negative Cutters. . . . . . Computamatch
                         Kerri Aungle
                       Veronica Marcarno
Video Conform . . . . . . True Media Ltd

Music Supervisors . . . .
            Becca Gatrell & Karen Elliott
               for Hothouse Music Ltd.
Music Editor. . . . . Tony Lewis
Music Recorded and Mixed by . . . .
               José Luis Crespo Dueñas
Music Recorded at. . . . .
                  Abbey Road Studios, London
Music Mixed at . . . Sphere Studios, London
Assistant Engineers . . . . Sam Okell
                         Rob Houston
                       Francesco Cameli
Orchestra Conductor . . . . Alberto Iglesias
Composer Management . . . .
            Ana Eusa & Javier Martín for RLM
Music Co-Produced by . . . . Javier Casado
Music Copyist . . . . Vic Fraser
Translator . . . . Cristina Aragon
Musician Contractor . . Isobel Griffiths Ltd.
Percussion Specialist . . . . . . Paul Clarvis
Nyatiti and Vocals. . . . . . . Ayub Ogada
Orchestra Leader . . . . . . Gavyn Wright

SOLOISTS

Turkish Clarinet/Nawala/Mizmar . . . . . .
                       Javier Paxariño
Guitar . . . . John Parricelli
Ronroco . . . . Javier Crespo
Accordion . . . . Javier Casado
Viola . . . . Yulia Malkova
Double Bass . . . . Chris Laurence
Marimba. . . . . Frank Ricotti
Harp . . . . Skaila Kanga
Cello . . . . David Daniels
Piano . . . . Simon Chamberlain

"Dicholo"
Written and Performed by Ayub Ogada
Mixed by Ben Findlay
Published by Womad Music Ltd.
(P) 2005 Real World Records Ltd./
Virgin Records Ltd.
Ayub Ogada appears courtesy of
Real World Records Ltd.

"Kijani Mwana Mwali"
Traditional
Performed by Bomas of Kenya
Taken from the Album
'Songs of African Heritage' EUCD1721
Courtesy of ARC Music
Productions International

"So Sei Viver No Samba"
Written by Ari Moraes
Performed by Cibelle
Published by Les Editions de la Bascule/
Strictly Confidential (BMI)
Under License from Ziriguiboom/
Crammed Discs
Courtesy of Six Degrees Records
By Arrangement with Ocean Park Music Group

"Kothbiro"
Written by Mbarak Achieng
Arranged and Performed by Ayub Ogada
Published by Womad Music Ltd./
EMI Virgin Music Ltd.
(P) 1993 Real World Records Ltd./
Virgin Records Ltd.
Ayub Ogada appears courtesy of
Real World Records Ltd.

"Happy Birthday to You"
Written by Patty Hill and Mildred Hill
Performed by Rachel Weisz
Published by EMI Music Publishing Ltd.

"Forever"
Written by Nazizi Hirgi/Kevin Waire/
Tedd Josiah
Performed by Necessary Noise
Published by Blu Zebra Music
Courtesy of Blu Zebra Records, Nairobi,
Kenya
Licensed by Arrangement with A.I. Records,
Nairobi, Kenya

**This Film is Dedicated to
YVETTE PIERPAOLI
AND ALL OTHER AID WORKERS
WHO LIVED AND DIED GIVING A
DAMN**

**Nobody in this story, and no outfit or
corporation, thank God, is based upon
an actual person or outfit in the real
world. But I can tell you this; as my
journey through the pharmaceutical
jungle progressed, I came to realize that,
by comparison with the reality,
my story was as tame as a
holiday postcard.
—John le Carré**

With Thanks to

The Kenyan Government
The British High Commission

The United Nations
The United Nations World Food Programme

The People of Kenya, particularly those from
Kibera, Loiyangalani, and El Molo
Catholic Mission Loiyangalani

The Kenya Police
Kenya Airports Authority
Nairobi City Council
Magadi Soda Company, Kenya
Ol Kedjiado County Council
Sudanese People's Liberation Movement
Buko Pharma-Kampagne

Original Pictures, Canada
Kim Todd
Ellen Rutter
Manitoba Film & Sound, Canada
Bradley Adams, Antonio Charlone, Sir
Edward Clay, Anne Clay, Jane Cornwell,
Dr. Jeremy Cotter, Eric Falt, Gustavo
Giandini Giani, Chris Gill, Ray Kyles,
Anna Grete Mason, Jason Matthus, Quico
Meirelles, Ciça Meirelles, Laura Melo,
Dr. Aisling Morris, Michael Murphey, Mark
Norton, Mike Rudell, Kitty Stanbrook,
Heather Stewart, Brian Woods

WFP/World Food Program
Dolby SR&SRD&DTS, in selected theatres

MPAA Rating: R (for language, some violent images, and sexual content/nudity)

Produced with the participation of the gov-
ernment of Manitoba
Manitoba Film and Video Production Tax
Credit

Made with the support of the National
Lottery through
the U.K. Film Council's Premiere Fund

Filmed entirely on location in Kenya, Sudan,
Germany, the U.K.,
and in the province of Manitoba, Canada

An Anglo-German Co-Production

Copyright © 2005 Focus Features LLC/Scion
Films
TCG Production Partnership/U.K. Film
Council
All Rights Reserved

Focus Features LLC/Scion Films TCG
Production Partnership/U.K. Film Council
are the authors of this motion picture for the
purposes of the Berne Convention and all
natural laws giving effect thereto.

The characters and incidents portrayed and
the names herein are fictitious and any simi-
larity to the name, character or history of any
actual persons living or dead is entirely coin-
cidental and unintentional.

This motion picture is protected under the
laws of the United States and other countries.
Unauthorized duplication, distribution or
exhibition may result in civil liability and
criminal prosecution.

No animals were harmed in the making of
this film.

www.theconstantgardener.com

Soundtrack available on Octave Music

A Focus Features Release

About the Contributors

JEFFREY CAINE (Screenplay)Born in London, Jeffrey Caine was educated at the Universities of Sussex and Leeds. He taught English in schools and colleges for four years before becoming a professional writer.

An author of scripts for television and film, Mr. Caine is also the author of several novels. One, *Heathcliff*, tells the story of the "missing" years of Emily Brontë's romantic hero, following his adventures in the criminal underworld of 18th-century London and his education there by a lady of fashion.

His television works include the police drama series *The Chief*, starring Tim Pigott-Smith and Martin Shaw, which ran successfully for five seasons on Britain's Independent Television network and for which, as writer and series creator, Mr. Caine was nominated for a British Television Society Award.

His screenplays include *GoldenEye*, directed by Martin Campbell, which established Pierce Brosnan as James Bond; and *Rory O'Shea Was Here*, directed by Damien O'Donnell and also released by Focus Features. The latter film won the Audience Award at the 2004 Edinburgh International Film Festival, and Mr. Caine was honored with the Irish Film and Television (IFTA) Award for Best Script.

JOHN le CARRÉ (Author)John le Carré is the *nom de plume* of David John Moore Cornwell, who was born in Poole, Dorset.

Mr. Cornwell was educated at Sherborne School, at the University of Berne (where he studied German literature for a year) and at Lincoln College, Oxford. He graduated from the latter with a first-class honors degree in modern languages.

He taught at Eton from 1956 to 1958, and was a member of the British Foreign Service from 1959 to 1964, serving first as Second Secretary in the British Embassy in Bonn and subsequently as Political Consul in Hamburg.

He started writing novels in 1961, and since then has published the following titles, nineteen in total: *Call for the Dead, A Murder of Quality, The Spy Who Came In from the Cold, The Looking Glass War, A Small Town in Germany, The Naïve and Sentimental Lover, Tinker Tailor Soldier Spy, The Honourable Schoolboy, Smiley's People, The Little Drummer Girl, A Perfect Spy,*

The Russia House, The Secret Pilgrim, The Night Manager, Our Game, The Tailor of Panama, Single & Single, The Constant Gardener, and *Absolute Friends.* Several of the novels have been made into film or television productions.

Mr. Cornwell is an Honorary Fellow of Lincoln College, Oxford, and has Honorary Doctorates at Exeter University, The University of St. Andrews, Bath University, The University of Southampton, and The University of Plymouth.